Young People's Parables

Young People's Parables

Edited by
Geoffrey Barlow

Quartet Books
London Melbourne New York

First published by Quartet Books Limited 1983
A member of the Namara Group
27/29 Goodge Street, London W1P 1FD

Copyright © 1983 by Geoffrey Barlow

British Library Cataloguing in Publication Data

Young people's parables.
   1. Children's writings, English
   2. English literature—20th century
   I. Barlow, Geoffrey
   820.8'09282   PR1110.C5

   ISBN 0-7043-3457-7

Typeset by MC Typeset, Chatham, Kent
Printed and bound in Great Britain
by Mackays of Chatham Ltd, Kent

Contents

Introduction

When I conceived the idea of a Literary Competition for Young Authors, under the auspices of the Church of England Children's Society, I never realized that it would create such interest. The standard of entries was high, and it was difficult for the judges and myself to select the final winners.

I am very much indebted to Malcolm Muggeridge, who acted as chairman of the judges and for the indispensable help and guidance that he has given me throughout the competition. I am extremely grateful to the judges, Basil Boothroyd, Rosemary Sutcliff, Robert McCrum, Max Le Grand, Peter Moss and Peter Shankland, and thank them for their unfailingly generous help. I am also grateful to Kitty Muggeridge for all the teas consumed during the period of the competition. A special thank you to Michael Aldridge and Marion Chamberlain, and the Directors and all the staff of the Church of England Children's Society.

Major contributions to the success of the competition were made by the following: Christina Foyle for allowing prizes to be presented at one of the famous Foyles Literary Luncheons, and Mr Perrick of W & G Foyle; BBC Radio Brighton for the use of their studios; Norman Wareham and Radio Kent; Stewart

Lamont and Ken Bruce of Radio Scotland; Naim Attallah and David Elliott of Quartet Books; Simon Wratten of Oxford University Press; my son Richard for all his help in the field of photography; and Peter Austin of the *Sussex Express*.

I say a special thank you to all the contestants, and congratulations to the winners. The competition is now an established event, and I hope that 1984 will bring a big crop of entries.

Geoffrey Barlow, Competition Secretary
East Hoathly, Sussex.
July, 1983

Letter from Malcolm Muggeridge to Geoffrey Barlow,
18 July, 1983

Dear Geoffrey,

Your daring adventure in young authorship, under the auspices of the Church of England Children's Society, has been a great success. Please accept my congratulations and thanks for being allowed to participate. Getting the entrants to undertake writing a parable at all was somewhat hazardous, but it worked. The parables submitted varied in quality, but the great m jority displayed awareness of what a parable is or aims at being – according to the Oxford Dictionary, 'Any story or narration in which something is expressed in terms of something else'.

It is a literary form which has always fascinated me, if only because Jesus used it almost exclusively in his teaching. That is to say, he was a story-teller of unique quality rather than any kind of guru, don or demagogue. In view of the ever-deepening mist of fantasy in which people live today, might not 'What I believe' or 'What is real?' provide a good theme for next year?

yours,

Malcolm Muggeridge

From Rosemary Sutcliff

We all know that the Parables are great truths and great moral precepts enshrined in stories so that we may be the more easily able to understand them.

Some of us cannot fully understand or accept them even so; (I personally have always had a strong sympathy with the son who stayed at home and worked the farm and did *not* get the fatted calf killed for him). But somewhere deep down inside us, even so, I think we all recognize that the great truths are there, even when we ourselves are not great enough or maybe simple enough for them. At any rate we can think about them and try to receive them, and that is what the tellers of these modern parables have done.

As a Teller of Tales myself, and one who tries to keep certain truths at the heart-core of the stories told, it has been such a delight to me to help judge the competition for which are the winning entries, and so, maybe, catch the first glimpses of those who will themselves be Tellers of Tales one day.

Rosemary Sutcliff
18 July, 1983

From Basil Boothroyd

It was amid the chandeliers and mirrored opulence of the Dorchester Hotel, at a Foyle's Literary Luncheon, that the winners of the competition received their prizes. The eating and drinking being over by then, I was in an amiable, not to say vulnerable, state of mind.

Organizers of charitable and similar altruistic ventures are practised in choosing their moment to strike. Geoffrey Barlow, organizer of this one, struck when my defences were down.

'Could you rattle off something for the front of the book?'

'No,' I said.

His genial smile dimmed a bit. Well, I had been blunt. But those of us who live by words are apt to take words literally. I didn't mean that I couldn't write something. Only that I couldn't rattle it off. The good, kind, charitable and altruistic Geoffrey, himself from time to time committed to the printed page, should have known this. Or he may be a rattler? I don't know. Writers tend to be too obsessed with, too painfully wrapped up in their own work methods, to concern themselves with other people's.

Rattlers there are, and I wish I were one of them. I think they must be the lucky exceptions, possessing that direct, effortless drive from the brain to the fingers to the flickering keyboard to the publisher to the printer to the page. I was going to add, 'to the public', but I thought about it for a time, some five or ten minutes, and decided I had enough p's already. And in the preceding paragraph – there we go again – I already have 'printed page': two more p's, and the word 'page' now repeating again . . . No, no. That is tautology. The word 'repeat' enshrines the word 'again'. Careless. Should I unpick the last dozen lines or so? It may not show, but I have unpicked them a couple of times already. After another five minutes' rattle-free silence I decide against it. I could rephrase that, because I've used the word 'decided' already, too recently for readers not to suspect a poverty of vocabulary; and, pardonably, by the look of this stuff so far.

I'm not at all happy about that word 'enshrines'. Would 'embraces' be better? 'Conveys'? A weak word.

I could start the whole thing again from the top. And avoid, among other clumsinesses, these two paragraphs both beginning with an 'I'.

I try to avoid that.

Good grief, now look what I've done.

But I've started the thing again from the top a couple of times already. Does it show? Does it matter? Do you, the reader, care that I have raided Dr Roget's *Thesaurus* for the perfect adjective, though never quite finding it, and all for a sentence that you may skip and never miss, just because the telephone rings, or a voice from the next room announces supper?

Or just because I've lost your attention anyway?

Should I chuck the whole project and go and sit in the sun, which shines so seductively in the garden outside?

No. I only have today to rattle this off. Tomorrow, latest, I must continue to rattle off a book. The publisher has been on several times lately. 'How's the book coming?' Books don't come. Publishers, and readers too, think they do. Or that is the impression received by those of us who live by words.

Words don't come. Words are gouged, prised, quarried. They fight every inch of the way.

The act of writing, the actual activity (goodness, that's terrible, 'act', 'actual', 'activity') is not a process recognized by readers. The blame for this lies with writers who write books about writers, in which the writers they write about never seem to do any writing, consequently having limitless time on their hands to pursue complicated love affairs. Or partly. The real trouble, giving rise to the calm assumption that anyone can write, and causing a writer's correspondents to flood him with racy letters studded with exclamation marks and clichés ('calm assumption' is a cliché!), is that anyone can write. Words, written or spoken, are the common currency of life, unlike the other arts; had we, from birth, communicated by painting and sculpture, music and mime, we should be aware of the daunting problems of the wordsmith, that rare practitioner in an art which we could barely contemplate as a field of our own expression.

As things are, articulate from birth – lumpy euphony there, 'are', 'articulate' – and able to set down on paper at an early age, such clear gems as, 'Dear Santa, I want a big Teddy', we feel that we are then more or less ready to write a book. Many, indeed, write books, who are barely qualified to write to Santa Claus.

Even in the course of this discourse I hear a lady singer being respectfully interviewed on the radio. 'They offered me, like, this great contract for my next album,' she is saying. 'But I said no, OK, stay out of the studios a couple months like, know what I mean, maybe write a book, kind of thing.'

Where is all this leading me? A question I often ask at this stage, as I put my fourth page of typewriting into the machine for the fifth time. If I can't answer, which often happens, I have to put the first page in again.

This I shall not do. It would result in a piece of good, anyway better, writing, with an appearance of flowing and effortless ease.

That would defeat the exercise. And what is that? It is a pretentious exercise. Let me say that before you do. And is addressed less to the readers than the writers of this book, like, kind of thing, know what I mean. To remind them, and others who wish, or are otherwise incited, to grapple, battle and subdue the printed word, that flowing and effortless ease is no part of this laborious process.

Some of those whose work follows will have discovered this already. Let them pass on what they have learnt. Adding perhaps, if only as a warning to lady singers between albums, a simple equation from a fellow-sufferer, for whom it has worked out pretty accurately over the years. One hour's writing = half a minute's reading.

Put it another way, rattling off isn't on.

Basil Boothroyd
18 July, 1983

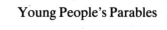

Young People's Parables

Freedom

For want of a better idea, Michael headed for the zoo. His normally aimless pace quickened now that he had a purpose, but his thin shoulders still hunched forward defensively inside his overcoat and his eyes watched the world with a painfully vulnerable expression, like a small hunted animal.

Michael had finally reached the conclusion that he was a total failure in life. Everywhere he saw people who seemed 'strong characters' – boys his own age, brimming with self-assurance and the arrogance of youth, people who knew their goal in life and set out with confident determination to reach it, his bold and witty schoolmates whom he envied so deeply, secure in their proud young independence and popularity. That left him, by his own comparison, a pale shadow, quiet and uninteresting, with no sparkling personality that he could discern, a poor conversationalist, easily and often viciously put down by his stronger-minded acquaintances, someone who could only trail meekly after the leaders, or walk alone – a weak character, in a fast-moving uncaring world that demanded strength and determination and the will to succeed, or else left you sinking in loneliness and despair: which Michael hopelessly believed was his fate. And so he walked on in the dragging quagmire of his self-pity, head down, his whole body seeming to shrink and flinch away from the cruel world he hated.

He reached the zoo, paid, and entered. He wandered around aimlessly, wrapped in his cold grey cloud. Then, coming to the big cats section, he stopped upon sighting a huge Bengal tiger lying in a corner of its cage. As he watched, the tiger rose and stood motionless apart from the tip of its tail, which twitched constantly, angrily. It was a picture of magnificence – big and immensely powerful, its tremendous strength evidently tightly restrained, and awe-inspiring – a king among animals, noble and majestic in bearing. Hot yellow eyes glaring its pride and arrogance, reflecting the security of invulnerability, its splendid coat flamboyant in glorious colour. Michael's bitter eyes absorbed all this and the contrast only disheartened him further.

Then the tiger moved. It paced slowly towards him, savage eyes staring. Its gait was smooth and lithe, muscles rippling beneath lustrous fur – and yet Michael was sure he could detect a strange aimlessness in its action. And then, like a ray of light piercing the black clouds in his mind, he understood. The mighty beast pressed its forehead against the bars and snarled softly – and, abruptly, the image of wild proud strength was gone, and all Michael could see in the gleaming eyes was a heartrendingly piteous expression of hopeless fury and despair. For this magnificent specimen of cruel and primitive power was behind bars, where its strength and beauty were useless to it – good only for its human jailers to stare at. And Michael saw that he had the one thing the tiger could no longer glory in – freedom.

He had to blink hard as, ashamed and humbled, he watched the imprisoned animal start to pace wearily round and round its bleak cage, past the unyielding bars that rendered its proud spirit impotent. As Michael hurried to the exit, his shoulders straightened, his head came up to face the world squarely at last, and his eyes brightened with fresh hope and resolve, for he was young and free and he had the chance to direct his life the way he wanted it. As he came out on to the street, he reflected that freedom is never truly valued until it is lost.

Anita Bailey (17)
Irthlingborough, Northants

Not by Works

A certain married couple wanted to adopt a child, so they went to visit the local children's home. They were determined to make the right choice of child to bring up and live with, so they went around the home talking to each child.

The very first child they met pleaded with them to be adopted: 'I would be really good around the house,' he said, 'I can clean, and wash up – and even cook. I would make sure that I earned my keep,' he went on.

The couple moved sadly to the next child.

'Why should I want to be adopted by you?' he said. 'I've got everything I want here; food, clothes, a bed, and soon I'll be able to stand on my own two feet!'

'But what about parents? Someone to love, and be loved by?' asked the mother.

'Who cares?' replied the boy: an attitude they met only too frequently, and were deeply saddened by.

The next child looked slightly older than the rest. 'I'm nearly sixteen,' he exclaimed. 'If you adopt me, in a few months I'll be able to go out and work, and then I'll be able to pay you weekly. A kind of repayment for taking me away from here!'

'How could you repay with money the love and care that we want to give you as parents?' asked the father.

Time after time, the children tried to give them good reasons why they should be adopted. But to the parents all these material intentions seemed like meagre, pathetic attempts to justify a position as a son or daughter. The father said: 'If we wanted a housekeeper, or a worker, then we would have to demand more than a pitiful token of work. We would have to ask for faultlessness, perfection, obedience, someone who could and would do everything for us.'

Naturally the children thought this was most unfair. 'Who do they think they are, coming along expecting us all to be perfect?' 'How can we possibly be so good?' 'They will be searching for a long time if they want to find someone perfect!' were typical comments.

The wife continued: 'All we want is someone to care for, someone to love – someone to make sacrifices for! We know that you can't be perfect, but any hopeless attempts at goodness or perfection are just a waste of time, a shadow of how you should be. Can't you see what we want?!'

The stunned stillness was broken by a young girl in a wheel-chair: 'Please adopt me,' she said. 'I can't even walk, let alone help you with the housework. All I want are real parents who I can love and be with, and be loved by. I can't live on my own – I need you! All I can give you is a pathetic love, in return for the great love of parents. Please take me.'

Guess who was adopted?

Anthony F. Heald (15)
Colne, Lancashire

Reality

The Bishop of — sat down to deafening applause from the audience at the opening of the new church, St Peter's in —. Nationally recognized both among laymen and fellow-ecclesiastics as one of the greatest and most active advocates for the Christian faith of modern times, he was regarded as a man who was as close to God as any Christian. In the eyes of everyone he was pious and devoted to his duty, but without seeming to make a great show of his respect and love for God, a man who had never spoken an angry word against anyone, nor acted in a way that was not in accordance with the Christian life that Christ had seen as the way to heaven.

Or so he appeared. And though he was a zealous and honest servant of God, he could not hide from himself that he in fact had never known God. However diligently and conscientiously he carried out his spiritual duties, or however strictly he disciplined himself, he was unable to find any contact with God, as if some infinitely deep void were between him and understanding God. There had always been a certain detachment in his prayers, a hidden obstacle to a meaningful and honest relationship with a person whom so many others had seen but who still eluded him.

He was becoming increasingly aware that his life was a pattern of rituals which for him had no purpose, no reason for their performance, and that his dedication to his position as a very active member of the Church was partly to disguise his spiritual inadequacy from himself, unsuccessfully, as his frequent but frustrated cross-examinations of himself had revealed.

In a US Federal Life-Internment Prison a killer was waiting for his death at the hands of human justice. He had been sentenced to death for the slaughter of two young families as they had met for an evening meal. He had done it, not for the money he might have gained from robbing them, but for a sadistic satiation of a momentary lust for blood. Looking back on the moment when he had gunned them down in a hail of bullets, oblivious to their screams and pleas, he knew he had been mad, he couldn't have done it if he was sane, honestly, he couldn't . . . Now the realization of what he had done and what was going to happen when dawn broke was starting to hit him, thudding with leaden blows into and through his skull. No one at that time, not even himself, had believed the plea he had made that he had killed when not in control of his mind. All he had now was knowledge that he was innocent – and that was all.

As he was led out of his cell, the sun had just risen above the far-off, serenely impassive hills. It would be a beautiful day – except he was condemned to lose the freedom of any appreciation or share of the inestimable yet so taken for granted pleasure in a new day. And then, just as his mind was at its lowest ebb of depression, he understood that he was not alone in the mental torment he was undergoing. As his eyes met the warm, fresh light of the sun which passed over the hills, he knew that someone else understood, that somehow he was experiencing a rebirth inside him, a new lease of life far beyond his fears of death. In that brief moment he had known God, and as the whiplash of the rifle reports cut through the cool morning air, he had passed into a further life where he was innocent of all he had committed in his previous life, a pilgrim who had finally reached his rest.

Piers McCleery (15)
Chobham, Surrey

On the Edge

'You've betrayed me.'

She unclenched her fist, and released the dead leaves she had held, watched them float gradually down on to the river below to land silently on the swirling water. Her young face was mirrored on the surface, and beside hers glimmered the face of an older man.

The mouth of the reflected face opened, and her father spoke: 'You can't say that. What I'm doing is the best for all of us, I'm sure. You must understand why I have to leave: I'm not doing this on impulse, you know – this is something that's been building up for some time. You can't say you haven't noticed.'

His memory reminded him of scenes he would rather forget. Oh yes, they had been happy enough at the start of marriage, but somehow it had tarnished with time. Their daughter had cemented them together again, for a while; but when they realized there could be no more, they both knew it was the end. He looked at his daughter, leaning on the edge of the bridge, still staring over into the water. Maybe she would never understand fully, he thought. He studied her outline, and saw the first hints of womanhood, and the face so like her mother's, his ex-wife's.

His daughter spoke, still staring at the water: 'Do you really think I could understand someone who betrayed the love of his family?' she murmured softly.

'Darling, there was no love between us at the end,' he answered tenderly. She stabbed a glance at him as the wind caught her hair, lashing it over her cheeks; the drizzle smudged her tear-stained face.

'I don't just mean Mum! What about me? I loved you too – isn't that enough? You can't just sweep me under the carpet, and walk off! You're too selfish, just thinking of yourself. Don't you see I still need you? Who can I turn to for help, if you've gone?'

The words pierced his composure, and bit into his confidence. He knew his answer was hollow: 'If it's money you mean, I'll keep you well supplied.'

Her answer was a stony gaze; she did not need to speak. Every minute she was learning new things about her father, things she had never thought she would see. The kind-hearted man, who had cherished her and coaxed her through her early years, had been replaced by a shivering coward.

'Anyhow, you'll still come to see me, won't you? We'll still be together, sometimes,' he said, plaintively. The very nature of the question betrayed his doubts; he got no answer. He knew she would blame him for destroying her life; she saw her security crumble around her, and the people she had trusted desert her. He wanted to hold her, ask for her forgiveness; help her to understand his actions. Yet she was still too young to catch more than an inkling of what was involved.

She turned to walk off the bridge, scooping up another handful of dead leaves as she went. She turned towards him, her face framed by her red hair – autumnal, like the tree beside her. As she stood there, the realization dawned on him – he had not expected this reaction from her. He did not know this young woman before him – now he never would.

Slowly she raised her head and released the leaves; the wind snatched them away. A last gesture perhaps – a last reckless act of passing youth. Now adulthood had been thrust upon her; the only example to follow was one of failure, set by her parents.

She walked away. Her father remained alone on the bridge. As he saw her disappear into the distance, a sudden doubt clutched his heart: had he been wrong? Should he have stayed with his wife – for his child's sake? He peered anxiously over the edge of the bridge, the old stonework crumbling in his grasp. The water seethed, and in the turmoil he saw, reflected, the turmoil in his heart. For one horrendous moment, the water beckoned him, offered an easy way out, an escape into oblivion. One short jump and it would all be over.

He turned to walk off the bridge, sweat on his forehead. For an instant, the water had seemed enticing, but now he realized he could not jump.

He was too much of a coward, even for that.

Adrian Newton (18)
Altrincham, Cheshire

My Dad's Bigger than Your Dad

Walking home from school one November day was a small boy. His clothing was suitable for the cold weather, yet it showed no sign of extravagance. Although clean and tidy, his clothes hung loosely on his slender body. As he stumbled along, weighty school bags becoming heavier with each step, he could hear the loud voices of several adolescent boys in the distance. As he approached them a lump formed in his throat. He bravely attempted to pass them with a lowered head, when his belongings were knocked to the ground. He looked up; his frightened eyes were met by jeering ones. The group of awkward-looking boys, only recently having come to puberty, surrounded him and began to shout obscenities. Then they began to play a childish game.

'Hey kid, where do you live?'

The boy answered timidly: 'Over there on the hill.'

'Over there, over there. Hey Gaz, did you hear that?'

Gaz was the leader of this pathetic group of gansters, the son of a wealthy garage-owner. He delighted in situations such as this.

'I bet my father's better than your father,' he shouted.

Taking offence, but avoiding an aggressive tone, the boy

calmly replied; 'Oh I'm sure he's not.'

'He's quite sure that he's not. Well, what have we got here?'

'Hit him Gaz, go on.'

'No wait, let's have a bit of fun. Look, kid.' Gaz gave him a push that made the boy lose his balance but did not make him fall over. 'I bet my house is bigger than yours, and I bet I get more money, and records, and I've got my own TV and radio and a bike. And I bet my father's better than yours.'

Now with a gleam of pride in his eyes the little boy replied: 'You might have more money than me, and have your own record-player, records, TV and bike, but your house isn't bigger than mine and your father isn't better than my father.'

'Oh no? Well if your house is so big then show me.'

'All right, if you want to see where I live I'll show you.'

The gang followed him curiously. They reached a large white gate and the boy stopped in front of it. The gang looked puzzled as the boy pointed to a large sign to the left of the gate. It read: 'ST ANN'S ORPHANAGE'.

A long white house showed through a patch of dormant trees and a ring of cheerful daffodils surrounded the building.

'But that's an orphanage.'

'Yes.'

'But if you live in an orphanage you can't have a father.'

'Yes I can.'

'Well, who is he?'

'God,' replied the boy.

And the gang watched in silence as the little boy walked proudly through the gate.

Glenda Rogers (15)
Rainhill, Merseyside

13

The Job Interview

Three men attended an interview for a job. One was dressed in a three-piece suit; his hair was neatly cut; he appeared to be everything an interviewer would look for in a prospective candidate. The second man was much more trendily dressed: as a concession to the occasion he had donned a tie so despite his slightly dyed hair, he was quite smart too. The third man sat on his chair uncomfortably. A week's stubble glistened on the end of his chin; his trousers were stained and his jacket torn; he warmed his hands on the bowl of his pipe.

Each man was called to the Director's office. To the first man the Chairman asked: 'Why do you want this job?'

The man answered that it would be the crowning achievement to years of hard work both at school and university. He had spent his life absorbed in study and he thought that he would be a great asset to any company.

The Chairman thought for a while, then he said: 'You have obviously spent all of your time quite absorbed in yourself – you spent your childhood indoors without friends or interests. Since you have put yourself before others and done nothing for society, what use could you be to my firm?'

Then he called in the second man and asked him why he wanted the job. This man said that he was really good with people, in fact he was a natural people's man! 'I am the life and soul of any party, the most popular boy at school, never short of a girlfriend, always out for a drink – any company would be lucky to have me working for them.'

The Chairman thought again and then said: 'You would be of no use to our firm either. Your life has been spent purely on pleasure, you have never considered anything seriously. You do not know what it means to work.'

Then the third man came forward, his worn boots shuffling across the floor, and the Chairman asked him in turn why he wanted the job.

'I have been made redundant and I cannot live without some means of employment. My family is hungry and I am prepared to try anything to support them. I realize that there is little I can do without training and, looking at those two fellows outside, I can't believe I have much chance, but I am prepared to learn. Until then I am willing to clean the floors or do anything that is useful so that I can earn an honest living.'

Again the Chairman thought for a while. 'This man has no qualifications, he is nothing, but how can I deny him a job when he comes to me on his hands and knees? He is open and honest, he presents himself to me as he is and nothing more.'

Christopher M.F. Hancock (15)
Kingston-upon-Thames, Surrey

A Modern Parable

It was cold and dank in the porch of the city church where the vagrant stood, swaying unsteadily and blowing into his grimy mittened hands. Flakes of plaster had fallen from the damp walls. At least it was not as cold there as in the street outside, where he had been ordered to move while the elegant congregation was hurrying into the church, searching in crocodile handbags and pigskin wallets for their gold-edged invitation cards. They shook the snowflakes off their thick coats and stamped it from their boots, finally settling themselves with happy bustle into the pews, waving and nodding to acquaintances across the nave.

As soon as the final late-comer had entered and was hurrying to his place, a verger had shut the church door, firmly. Almost immediately a further flurry of snow had begun to fall, blowing into the porch, and the vagrant had retreated hastily into a far corner. Now he was sheltered from the wind and snow, but not from the intense December cold. From across the street, a policeman, himself sheltering in a shop doorway, stared at the tramp, and then spoke into his radio. The tramp moved hurriedly behind the large 'Entry by Ticket Only' sign standing at the church entrance. After a few more words into his radio, the policeman, evidently reluctant to cross the street in the driving snow, moved on down the pavement to the next shop doorway.

The tramp returned at once to the shelter of the church porch. Sometimes the sound of the wind outside, as it whistled around the city buildings, would die away briefly, and then the vagrant could hear snatches of the service going on inside the church – sometimes music from a sonorous organ, then gusts of festive song, and occasionally a voice. Once someone said: 'For there was no room for them in the inn.' At one point the wind dropped completely, and some of the words of the sermon reached the listener outside. 'Should be thinking . . . at this time . . . less fortunate than ourselves . . . brotherhood . . . loving our neighbour . . . charity . . . collection-plates.' And then the howling wind started up again, drowning the next burst of organ music.

A blessing, a final silence, and then the heavy door was opened. The tramp edged painfully into the corner as the congregation, pulling on thick coats and opening umbrellas, came, flushed and laughing, out past him into the sweeping snow. The wind was whirling the snowflakes around, lifting them up towards the heavy grey skies. With happy seasonal talk of gifts still to be wrapped and family and friends expected hourly, the congregation hurried out and away. No one cared to linger in the porch; everyone swept out into the blizzard, leaving the vagrant cowering like a leper in his corner. He savoured the current of warm air from the interior of the church, and the rich, festive odours of cigars and scent until, a few minutes later, the door had been firmly locked, and he was alone in the street.

Arnold Hunt (14)
Hendon, London

Heaven and Hell

The door creaked open. Through the blizzard she could just
make out the figures of two small children coming her way. She
shut the door quickly, not wanting them to know she was in
because she didn't want them knocking at the door and asking to
come in and warm themselves. She'd had kids do that before in
this kind of weather but she always turned them away because
she hated kids. Mostly, though, she would pretend she wasn't in
because she felt guilty at turning them away in such awful
weather.

There was a knock at the door and she ducked down behind
the table so that they wouldn't be able to see her if they looked
through the window. They knocked again. She kept quite still.
Then she heard them singing. She shuddered. She couldn't quite
make out the words they were saying but she couldn't hold out
any longer – she had to open the door. She pulled it slowly open
and saw two small boys standing there. Their faces looked alike
but that was all. One of the boys had pure white hair the colour of
fresh snow and his eyes were bright blue. He wore a white shirt
and white trousers but his feet were bare. The other boy's hair
was pitch-black and his eyes were dark green. He wore a black

shirt and black trousers, but again his feet were bare.

'It's ever so cold out here,' said the fair-haired boy. 'Could we come in and warm ourselves by your fire, please?'

'You're not coming in 'ere and disturbing an old lady of 'er peace and quiet,' she said sternly.

She went to shut the door but the dark-haired boy leaned on it to stop her.

'You either let us in or I'll hold the door open and you'll freeze with us,' he warned.

She moved out of the way and the boys came in and shut the door.

'You're a kind lady,' smiled the fair-haired boy.

'Be quiet,' snarled the old lady. 'I told you you would disturb me, didn't I?'

The dark-haired boy licked his fingers and drew a 'one' in the air, smirking.

'Yours is the only house for miles,' began the fair boy again.

'Shut up! You're disturbing me again. As soon as this blizzard shows any sign of stopping, you're going,' she snapped.

'But we'll freeze,' complained the fair boy.

'Oh 'ell!' she groaned.,

'Yes?' answered the dark boy.

'What?' she said, puzzled.

'I'm Hell,' he said, grinning.

'Heaven help me,' she said. 'Now you're playing tricks on me.'

'I can't help now,' the blond boy said. 'I gave you a chance but Hell won again.'

Suddenly the old lady grew horns. There was a flash of lightning and she and the dark-haired boy disappeared together. The fair-haired boy sighed.

'Hell can't always win,' he said. 'One day someone will grow wings. One day.' And he disappeared in a shower of stars.

Michelle Drapeau (14)
Welwyn Garden City, Hertfordshire

The Cash Nexus

One day, a man decided to give his three sons, all in their twenties, some money, to see what they could do with it in two years. To his oldest son he gave £5,000, to his second oldest £4,000, and to his youngest £3,000.

The oldest son formed a company with his £5,000, which throve and did a lot of successful business. By the end of the two years, he had made a further £10,000, which represents an annual increase of seventy-three per cent.

The second son invested his money in a building society, and received only ten per cent, bringing his total to £4,840. However, he had no chance of losing his money, unlike his older brother, who might easily have failed in his private enterprise, and lost all his father had given him.

The third son thought of a very good thing to do with his £3,000: he had seen a horse in a race with odds 43–1. This meant that if he staked £3,000, he could get back £132,000! He eagerly backed the horse, confident in his business sense and mathematics. Unfortunately, when the day of the race came, the horse only came second, so he lost all the money. This represents an annual increase of minus one hundred per cent.

When the father asked his sons what the money had turned into at the end of the two years, the oldest son showed him his bank balance, showing £15,000 in the bank. The father was delighted, and said: 'Keep the money, you have used it well.' The second son showed his building-society book, with its £4,840. The father was pleased, but not nearly as much as for the first son. He told the second son also to keep his money. When the youngest son showed his father his betting slip with '£3,000' on the back, he was very afraid. However his father understood and comforted him. The father then got out his cheque book and wrote out a cheque for £10,000, which he gave to the youngest son, saying, 'Don't use this for betting, but invest it in something like your brothers did. That's the way to get rich. You can only lose, never win, on the bookies.'

The two older sons were very annoyed about this, and protested in the strongest possible terms to their father. The father, however, just said, 'It is not the healthy men who need a doctor, but the sick,' and left.

Hugh Pritchard (15)
Whitstable, Kent

Parable of Youth

An old lady went into a shopping precinct to do the shopping for the week. She was with her husband. By the time she had bought the food and checked the receipt, it was dark. Her husband walked on ahead of her to fetch the car. He was going to meet her at the end of the subway.

She had two heavy bags to carry and walked very slowly along the dimly lit subway. Suddenly, she heard footsteps and voices behind her. As she turned around, a gang of youths grabbed her bags. Two of them beat her until she lay in a pool of blood in the gutter.

After about five minutes, a man walked along the subway. He saw the old woman and called the police. She was taken to hospital where she recovered gradually.

The woman was in hospital for two weeks when she had a visitor. A young man said he had seen the report in the paper. He wanted to prove that not all young people are bad. This man helped her recover. He also helped her learn to trust other people again, especially the young. The two soon became great friends and she began to think of him as her son. Even after she left hospital, he would come and visit her.

The police continued to look for the youths. Eventually a similar attack took place, but only one youth was involved. He told the police who attacked the old lady. The woman felt strong enough to identify them. One of the boys, she recognized, had visited her in hospital. She felt sad that he had deceived her but did not want to harm his future any more. The police told her she could not drop the charges because they had become involved. She decided not to give evidence. So because of lack of evidence, the case was dismissed.

Caroline Davey (14)
Bournemouth, Dorset

The Parable of the Packet of Seeds

Once a little girl went out and bought a packet of seeds. She had been looking forward to this, as her father had just given her a small patch of flowerbed of her own, and a shelf in the greenhouse, so she was very excited. She had to bicycle about one and a half miles to the local farm shop and when she got there she asked for a very big mixed packet of seeds. They had told her they didn't have that, but as she looked so disappointed they mixed her a packet specially, and she proudly paid.

When she got home, she immediately found her father and asked him to help her plant them. He told her, that as all the seeds were different, they would have to be planted in different ways. She emptied the packet on to a tray, and her father helped her to sort them out to the best of his knowledge. They put them into groups according to how they would be planted, and set to work. It ended up that half were planted outside in her flowerbed, and the other half in pots on her shelf in the greenhouse, as they were not such hardy seeds.

After about three months they all began to show as little green shoots, all exactly the same. The little girl was rather disappointed. However, later that month, little buds began to appear, and that summer they all bloomed into beautiful flowers. All different colours, shapes, sizes and smells. Some were tall, some were short, some spread out sideways. They were all different colours and shades the little girl had never imagined could be so beautiful. Some outside even had butterflies and bees around or on them, making them even more beautiful. But the little girl liked them all the same.

The moral of this story is that everybody is different, and brought up in different ways, having more advantages than others. Some are prettier, or have more gifts, but God loves them all the same. Whatever they're like, wherever they come from, however, they're treated, or whatever they've done.

Candida Smith (15)
Ashford, Kent

The Foolish Gardeners

Was it a fickle whim of chance which led the family along the narrow twisting lane to the little rose-clad cottage, crouching shyly under a canopy of sheltering oaks? The 'For Sale' notice was almost hidden beneath a cascade of sweet-smelling honeysuckle. The family was captivated and decided immediately that their search was over.

The cottage was a dream, the garden a fairy tale. Bending willows encircled a living pond, reaching down into its cool, green waters. Suddenly a kingfisher, splendid in its jewelled plumage, skimmed the surface of the pond, diving low to retrieve a tasty morsel, and then just as suddenly, dazzled into the evening sunset and was gone. Splashing ducks quacked a lively farewell to this familiar but fleeting visitor. Mayflies darted the still air and frogs croaked in the reeds below. Butterflies drank thirstily from the acquiescent foxgloves, and all the while bees hummed a lazy lullaby.

As the seasons came and went, the family marvelled at the effect of each on their garden: the birth of spring with the freshness of new life; the glorious splendour of summer; the mellow colours and veiling mists of autumn; the stark beauty of the winter landscape. The family became familiar with this abiding beauty, and complacent, caring less and less for the burden of guardianship which they had so eagerly accepted.

And then one cold winter's day, as nature slept and the naked trees reached silently to the leaden sky, the family decided to have done with the pond. They would cut down the creaking willows, drain the water and replace it with a summer house. The ancient copper beech was also to fall victim to their ruthless axe. During the long winter months they worked hard and by early spring the summer house was finished: a magnificent edifice as a tribute to their labours. They painted it in bright colours and furnished it with contemporary seats and cushions.

Then one hot day, as they sat in the summer house with the uninterrupted sun pouring in through the glass roof, they began to ask one another what was missing. Only then did they realize, too late, what they had lost. It was the beauty of this place with which they had fallen in love when they first chanced upon it. They had destroyed it for ever with their own hands. They remembered the spring with its primroses and bluebells, sheltering in the shade of the cool willows, and the calling birds as they nested in the hedges which once grew where the tall overlap fences now stood. The tap, tap, tap, of the busy woodpecker in the old ivy-clad elm tree, which once stood beside the pond, had long ceased. The vivid purples, blues and reds of the wild foxgloves, a haven for the many butterflies which once visited the garden, were now cleared to make room for the patio. And what of the family of hedgehogs who, as if by magic, appeared each evening from the undergrowth which once was? All gone, all destroyed, for ever. It was no longer the natural sanctuary, the place of enchantment. Instead, it was their own stark creation which did not take account of the beauty of nature and the birds, the insects and the animals whose home it had been also, and who, for so long, had shared it happily with man.

Caroline Ward (15)
Yeovil, Somerset

The Parable of the Paranoid Polyp

Among the pinnacles and towers of the Great Barrier Reef, untold millions of tiny coral polyps dedicate their lives to secreting lime, and when they die, their descendants continue above what they have built. This has been so since the dawn of Time, until the Great Mistake.

'Good Heavens!' exclaimed the Infinite Being, 'who let a four-mega-splurge intellect be created as a polyp? This kid should have been a human at least, if not a peri-Galactic Zaleptron. Gabriel, go and retrieve him and we'll convert him. And whoever it was, don't do it again.'

So, Jacob the Polyp was sought out by Gabriel, and summoned to stand before the celestial Throne.

The Creator knows some useful things about creatures. This may explain why the next few minutes had a sensible, Being-to-Being air about them.

'I'm sorry for the inconvenience,' apologized the Eternal. 'There's been a slight miscalculation here which resulted in your being brought to life as a polyp, when you are far too intelligent.'

Jacob made a timid, well-mannered remark to the effect that he hadn't noticed.

'What? Of course you are, son, believe Me. Now I'm promoting you to human being. I realize the transition could be depressing, but we can ease it for you by insulting your intelligence a teeny bit. That makes you mentally a human adult, OK? Now, Gabriel has your papers, (bureaucracy is humankind's fate, One feels), and he'll beam you down when you're ready. Any questions?'

'Is it going to be nice?'

'Er- depends what you mean by "nice". I'm with you if you want Me; just call Me, any time.'

So Jacob was restored to Earth, where he doubtless took up employment as a civil servant. From then on it should have been plain sailing, but for the cruel burden of natural weakness which enslaves us to eternity. You see (if you are human you probably know already), the human notion of living together is very different from the polyp nation. Although humans cannot exist by themselves, and are dependent on each other from the cradle to the grave, they won't admit it. They prefer to show some 'independence'. And it's this something-for-nothing attitude which Jacob was, sadly, too weak to swallow.

And as time went on, Jacob's excitement turned to disillusion. He watched the incredible power-struggles, the extravagant abuse of invaluable people, and the mindless aggression to which humans subject themselves, in the name of independence.

'I thought these people were intelligent,' he said. 'I said, I thought You said these people were intelligent.'

Apologizing to one's own creation is like having to go back for something one is sure one has not forgotten. Know the feeling?

'I was afraid you might find human society rather shocking. It's your coral background, you see. Can't change that now – well, I can, but it's Against My Principles.'

'Oh dear. It wouldn't perhaps be possible for me to be run

over? I'd really love to die – not meaning to be ungrateful I mean.'

So the Almighty turned up the warmth and sympathy until Jacob was flooded through. 'Tell you what. How would you like to be a marine biologist?'

'Would I? Listen, Father, You have real talent, You know that? You should have been an arbitrator.'

So, Jacob joined the Marine Exploratory Institute and had a whale of a time – I beg your pardon – except for the jellyfish. Of course, jellyfish intend no malice when defending themselves, but it's still painful to step on one.

The other marine biologists rushed to Jacob's rescue, and by their prompt aid they literally saved his life. Their attention and worry were new Freud to Jacob.

While Jacob was recovering, who should visit him but the Omnipresent. They got talking about research and Jacob said he'd discovered something about humans.

'Danger and suffering make them pull together like – like coral polyps!' smiled Jacob. 'You know, Lord, You ought to try that sometime – for our own good of course.'

One cannot venture to guess what is in the Mind of the Mindful One, but it is possible that He felt very old, just then. 'Oh, no,' He pleaded, 'not again!'

He/She who has forty-six chromosomes, let him/her hear. For I tell you that we are not too wise to learn from our cousins who built the Great Barrier Reef.

Elionar Adelson (18)
Hornby, Lancashire

No Gift to Offer

Imagine for a moment looking down at a carpet of swaying trees, at a forest near a wave-fringed coastline. Then draw nearer and peer down into an almost hidden glade covered in moss and encircled by tall, sturdy trees. Here, long ago, under an old pine, grew a little flower, whose pure white leaves framed a centre of flaming yellow.

Sadly this little flower was excluded from the activity of the glade and her faint comments went unheeded as the trees debated and discussed the matters of the day. The birds used to bring news from further afield, telling of village life, of the open sea and of the King who reigned over the land. As the birds chattered above, the flower listened in. She especially liked to hear how the King had once come and visited the forest, and she wished desperately that she too could fly over the King's castle.

Then one day there was extra disturbance in the glade. The trees swayed from side to side and the birds twittered from one branch to another. Everything was in a commotion. Straining, the little flower tried to hear what was happening but all in vain. Not until a plump robin had kindly hopped up to her and chirped:

'The King is coming, the King is coming,' did she realize that her greatest dream of seeing the King might come true. All the other plants and animals were just as excited, and soon plans were being formed and decisions being made as to what they would do when the King rode past.

In the treetops the birds' choir began to practise. At first there were a lot of wrong chords but under the wise owl's careful conducting a sweet sound soon filled the air. The pine trees decided to lay a soft carpet of needles, while the squirrels rushed from one end of the glade to another carrying armfuls of nuts as a present. In the midst of all this activity a silver birch began to taunt the little flower.

'What can a flower offer the King?' she mocked as her branches shook with laughter. Naturally this made the flower very miserable. Her petals drooped, her leaves wilted, for she knew there was really nothing she could give.

Suddenly from afar a bugle sounded as a last warning of the King's imminent arrival. So everyone made their final preparations and waited breathlessly.

Their wait did not last long, as through the trees rode the King, mounted on a silky black horse and followed by a procession of richly dressed noblemen. With a swish the trees bowed down yet the birds remained silent, paying homage to this young and handsome lord. At that moment the sun suddenly moved from behind a cloud and a shaft of light streamed down through the branches. As it did so the King dismounted, moving into the glade where everything stood still in anticipation. However, he hardly noticed the carpet of pine needles but bent instead to view the little flower.

Only the King had seen the sunlight fall and illuminate her delicate petals. Only this flower, so conscious of her frailty, had held his attention, not because of the great gift she had to offer but rather because she stood still ready to reflect the greatness of the sun.

Catherine Gammon (17)
Wimborne, Dorset

The Diamond

It was the biggest diamond to which the Azulo mine had ever given birth. The mineralogists all agreed it had been given the potential to be one of the most beautiful things in the world. As of the moment, it was still rough and uncut, but it shone as if it imprisoned the light of a hundred suns. The light emitted was pure white and dazzled its beholder. Its potential was limitless.

The mine owners decided to have the crystal cut into two separate diamonds, both being sold to different buyers. The cutter chosen for cutting such a superb gem was named Mr Life.

When it reached the cutter it surpassed even his expectations. Mr Life was eager to start his work and almost immediately started working out his plans on how to cut this marvel. The first task was to find a plane so that he would be able to cut the crystal exactly in half. It was almost flawless and so it took the cutter only a short time to draw up blueprints of how and where he must strike.

The day finally came when Mr Life took his chisel and mallet and made that first strike. The mallet came down with a crack like a whip breaking through the air, then silence. The diamond was split in two perfect halves. Mr Life smiled to himself – the diamond's history had begun. He was to mould it into what he wanted; this diamond had guidelines, but its potential to be brilliant was infinite.

Mr Life decided to cut both crystals exactly the same way, and so form a set which would be even more valuable. One half was placed on his workbench and Mr Life began to cut. At each stroke of the mallet another fragment of crystal fell away to reveal a smooth plane that shone and sparkled like a mountain stream which has caught the sun's first rays. The diamond was taking shape. It did not fault or crack, but with each stroke became more and more perfect. Then after many hours of painstaking work, Mr Life gave the final stroke; the diamond was truly brilliant, its many facets gleamed and even seemed to wink at Mr Life as if thanking him for what he had done. Mr Life spoke back as if it were alive, saying it had not been his doing, but that it was the diamond's own flawlessness that had prevailed. The diamond had stood the test. He was so pleased with himself and his creation that he wanted to start immediately on the diamond's brother, but now, he must wait for he knew that in his excitement he might make a mistake and the brother would be lost.

So Mr Life, after creating a masterpiece, went to bed. Of course he could not sleep; who could? He lay awake and thought of his day's work yet to come. In the morning he woke especially early and went straight to his workshop. Once again, as the day before, he placed the crystal to be cut on to his workbench. It too gleamed and shone even though it had not yet been cut. Mr Life smiled and sang to himself as he cut at the crystal; it had become almost like a sun. Then all of a sudden a fault showed up; it traversed the diamond and Mr Life was horror-stricken – he could not believe his eyes. How could something so perfect have a weakness? He hoped it would not crack and that in some way he could salvage it. However, with each stroke, Mr Life saw the weakness grow as if some evil force worked to force his diamond apart. Then on one of the strokes it happened – the diamond shattered. The weakness had grown too great and it had fallen. Mr Life looked at it, the broken pieces gleaming only slightly now, and it seemed to him a darkness was the centre for the shattered pieces. There was a knock on his door. He knew who it would be: another owner with another diamond.

Peter Resteghini (15)
Morpeth, Northumberland

The Believer

The ray of sunlight filtered through the window and danced across Mr Jesum's handsome face. Ann yawned; she hated assembly. RS wasn't too bad because then she didn't have to share Mr Jesum with five hundred other children. He was always so calm and kind, he never treated her as a troublemaker, not like the other teachers did. He was so strange – he'd appeared as if out of nowhere. Ann brought herself out of her daydream. 'And so the moral of today's story is that Jesus always looks after his children no matter what they have done.'

Ann yawned again. 'What a load of rubbish,' she whispered to Kelly who was sat next to her. 'He never looked after me when I was caught stealing and me Dad gave me a hiding.' Kelly giggled.

The rest of the day went fairly quickly, but then Wednesdays always did for Ann; she always looked forward to the Dance Club at the end of the day.

Ann wasn't very good academically but she certainly could dance. It was the only time she got praised. Tonight, though, was an exception. The dance teacher seemed to think Ann danced like an elephant and shouted at her constantly. Ann left the class miserable and dejected.

It was dark outside and cold; Ann pulled the collar of her coat up tightly around her and began to walk home. She hated the dark – it was like a large black blanket that covered everything – she always felt nervous. Ann turned the corner. Suddenly she heard footsteps behind her. She quickened her pace. The footsteps quickened also. Ann became very nervous; she could feel her heart beating faster and faster. Suddenly she broke into a run. The person behind her was running also. Ann turned another corner, panting and frightened.

A scream passed her lips as she collided with a man. She turned to run again but a hand held her tightly. Ann screamed again, but suddenly the calm familiar voice of Mr Jesum reached her ears. Ann relaxed.

'Someone was following me,' Ann said, panting.

'I know, I saw him and I thought you may need help,' Mr Jesum replied. 'I'll walk you home.'

Ann smiled. She didn't want to continue her journey alone.

'You know Ann, you're not a bad girl.'

Ann stared at her feet. 'Everyone tells me I am, and they don't give me a chance to prove that I'm not.'

Mr Jesum laughed. 'You think they don't but you have got a very important friend.'

It was Ann's turn to laugh. 'An RS teacher. Me Dad would laugh 'imself silly if I told 'im.'

They were now standing outside Ann's gate.

'Well, thanks for walking me home,' she said.

Mr Jesum smiled. 'Just remember I look after all my children no matter what they have done.'

Mr Jesum turned and left. But as he did so, Ann thought she saw him glow as though above his head there was a halo. Ann shrugged her shoulders and went in.

The next day Ann was met at the school gates by an excited

Kelly. 'Have you heard? Mr Jesum disappeared, vanished as if into thin air.'

Ann stared at Kelly. 'When was he meant to 'ave disappeared?'

'The headmaster said yesterday morning straight after Assembly. They think he's dead.'

Ann stared at the sun which shone brightly down on her.

'No,' she said, 'he'll never die. Jesus looks after his children no matter what they've done.'

Sharon Breach (17)
Ipswich, Suffolk

A Lightning Judge

A man stood to be judged before a court of law. His accuser pointed a finger at the man and said: 'This is the man. Only that which is true shall pass beyond my lips, and that I do swear to God.'

The judged turned to the accused. 'It is a serious crime that you are charged with; the penalty for being found guilty is death. Do you plead guilty or not guilty?'

'Not guilty my lord,' replied the man in the dock.

Outside the storm continued to vent its fury on the world in an obsessed, almost vindictive manner. The golden tongues of forked light speared the sky as though trying to carve it into smaller pieces.

The rain lashed down at deadly velocity, creating the same effect as a hail of bullets on the ground below, already submerged beneath mounting inches of icy wetness.

The wind seized command, taking a firm grasp of the storm. It hurled its comrades-in-arms about, casting stinging rain and flickering lethal charges into every available space. It also made available that which was not.

Inside, huddled beneath the relative safety of the stone and mortar building, the court session continued irrespective of the raging elements.

The jury processed evidence and analysed the facts; their decision did not lie far away.

Without warning, the ceiling suddenly became caught up in the centrifugal force of gravity. Down it rained on to the waiting heads of those trapped below.

Without hesitation the man in the dock leapt into action. Not in order to effect his escape, but to the aid of those less fortunate than himself, those who lay sandwiched between the floor and the fallen stone.

Among those he helped back on to their feet and to safety during the stone rain was the man who had sworn to see him hang.

When at last a semi-restored court stood ready to announce their verdict the judge spoke. 'He who is willing to cast aside thoughts of his own safety for those of others is welcomed within our world. But he who is willing to sacrifice his life to aid one who would see him die is honouring us by standing among us. I see no reason why such a man should pay the price after taking such risks without taking into account the cost. You are now a free man, go and show others that neighbours and enemies do not always wear recognizable colours.'

Sarah Lavender (15)
Chester, Cheshire

A Parable to Show God's Love

'So hear me, hear me when I tell you I am God. Let me help you understand.'

And he went on to say: 'Once there was a man whose son was due to be hanged for treason against the king of that country. The father took his son's place, yet even after the bloodthirsty crowd had seen him die, they still held a grudge against the son, who was eventually exiled. So was the father right to take his son's place, or was his dying in vain? I too had a son. They killed him you know. Let's just say I am the Father, a timelord perhaps, but rest assured that I *am* God. I even have my passport as proof. Why then do you not believe me? For if Joe Bloggs was to show you his identity, you would believe him. Are you perhaps afraid *because* I am God?'

The latest computer data on this weird man, who claims to be God, has shocked scientists, who believe the computer program to be of a faulty standard because it too claims this man to be God! More news from the BBC Newsroom follows shortly.

'I have proved, against your computers, to be acceptable to the character of God. Still you do not believe me. Yes, yes, you are afraid of me, but I am here for one purpose only and that is to propose multilateral nuclear disarmament. You are making dead people of yourselves.'

'Rubbish! He must have been sent from Russia as a decoy for our Master Computers. What would *he* know about nuclear weapons, even if he was God? Anyway, if he *is* God, what took him so long to get here?'

At this, the frail old man fell to the ground. 'I gave you a chance, a chance to believe. You took it from yourselves, and in return I take you, but at war, not peace.' With this final speech, the frail old man lay down, closed his eyes, and looked totally at peace with himself.

A stir in the crowd, and a woman came over. She knelt beside him. 'Whatever you are, you must be God. So peaceful, so loving and thoughtful. You *are* God but is it too late?' whispered the woman.

Just then a flicker of hope crossed the old man's face.

'Nah! He's no God! Just a senile old man. Should be locked away if you ask me!'

Tears in her eyes, the woman clutched hold of his hand. 'Sorry.'

'Nuclear weapons will destroy *my* world. I tried to stop you, to save my world, *and* them. I too am sorry.'

With that the old man simply dispersed into thin air. Yes, that's what I said, just disappeared. Pardon? Er . . . we have an urgent newsflash . . .

'RUSSIA HAS SET OFF HER NUCLEAR MISSILES. THEY ARE AIMED DIRECTLY AT LONDON!'

'You knew, you tried to prevent this, but be at peace with yourself; it is our fault,' was all the woman could say before she too dispersed into thin air.

Nicola Wright (14)
Bournemouth, Dorset

The Parable of the Foul Deed

Around the edge of the lake the water lapped disconsolately. Life had come to an abrupt halt for the infant now being dragged down into the waste which society had left under the cover of the wash of ages.

The young mother gazed at the sinking form with relief. She had felt that she would never rid herself of the child. Now the nightmare was over. She was a free woman once more. The only symbol of her guilt was being dragged into the murky depths by the dampening clothes in which it was swathed. The young woman no longer felt that she had anything to hide – the lake was hiding it for her. Or was it? Breathing in short gasps, she scoured the surface of the lake with her eyes. Was that blood on the surface? No, of course not, her imagination was running away with her. She had been so very careful not to pierce the child's skin that the blood could only exist in her mind's eye. It was merely that she associated water and blood with the death of innocents.

She was only too glad to get away from the lake and lock herself in her room. She had washed her hands of the matter, metaphorically speaking. Literally, however, she had not been able to face soaking herself in the bath. The young woman told herself continually that she had no cause to feel guilty – after all, the child's coming into the world at all had been a mistake and she was merely rectifying the error – yet she could not feel easy bearing the yoke of her knowledge.

Her conscience was the only thing that knocked at the door of her heart that night.

It was several days later that the Inspector called.

'Excuse me, miss, but there is something which I would like to talk to you about.'

She kept the door on the chain, wary of allowing anyone a glimpse into the interior of her citadel.

'Could I come in for a few minutes, miss?'

Slowly the door opened. Light flooded into the girl's face, its sheer intensity making her blink, while round the head of the Inspector it glowed like a halo.

'The body of an innocent child, nothing more than a babe in arms, has been found. Do you know anything about this?'

The young woman gasped and gave an exclamation of sincere surprise. How could he know about the child? She had dumped it in the lake, hidden from the eyes of the world.

'The child's body rose to the surface of the lake yesterday morning. It is believed that he had been "dumped".' The Inspector choked on the last word.

Realization of what she had done dawned on the woman and the emotions which she had been bottling up inside her came bursting forth.

Laying his hand on the shoulder of the woman who cowered to his left, the Inspector gazed at her with compassionate eyes.

'*Foul deeds will rise,*' he said.

Eleanor Whittaker (17)
Leicester

More is Not Enough

John was sitting sleepily at the breakfast table reluctantly eating the breakfast his wife had made him. He was just bringing the rim of his cup up to his lips when he saw the premium-bond results. He put his cup down suddenly in disbelief. But there it was, A 130568, the number he had. He had won two hundred thousand pounds, after years of nothing. He jumped up, kissed his wife and ran out of the front door to the post office as his wife sat, confused and bewildered.

After a quarter of an hour, John came back into the house panting. He showed the cheque to his wife, who suddenly understood as her mouth fell open.

The next day, John and his wife were up in London. The first shop they went to was a furniture shop. As John and his wife wandered around the shop, they saw that they could buy absolutely anything in it. After about half an hour of browsing the couple decided to see what else there was to buy in London.

The couple's next stop was a hi-fi shop. They saw, as before, that they could buy anything in the shop. A strange feeling was coming over them, beginning to replace the feeling of excitement they had had since the day before. The feeling was not a very pleasant one, just rather depressing. The couple moved on to the next shop, an antique shop. Here, again, they could buy anything they wanted. The new unpleasant feeling became more apparent now and the couple realized what it was. They realized that the fact that they could buy practically anything they wanted had made them feel no happier; the challenge had been lost. It was no longer a matter of getting the best for the money, but just the best. It was so easy, too easy. Before, they had yearned for the things that they could now buy, but they had got the money so suddenly. If John had worked and built it up over the years, that would have been fine, but they had made no plans and it was by pure chance that he had got the money.

When they went out of the antique shop, the couple looked at each other and wondered whether they really wanted the money. They walked down the street feeling unsatisfied and uncomfortable. Where was the challenge?

Soon, the couple passed a church, and John got an idea. He looked towards his wife, and she nodded. He took the cheque out of his inner pocket, put it face down against the wall, took out a pen and wrote on the back, 'Pay St Mary's Church, Westminster, John Cartright,' and slipped it into the donations box in the church wall. The couple walked slowly to the tube station, two hundred thousand pounds shorter but happier.

Christian Brindley (14)
Westbourne, Hampshire

The Newspaper Boy

It was an early October morning. The streets were nearly deserted, except for the two newspaper delivery boys, about to begin their rounds. Their conversation was as crisp as the morning air.

'Work at Malans? Andy, we can't!' Mark looked at his friend with disbelief.

'Why not? It's the same job, and nearly twice as much money. Just think. Don't you want more money?'

'Course I do,' replied Mark. 'But we all promised not to go near the place. Remember?'

They had promised to boycott the shop as revenge for the humiliation of one of their friends, Richard. The shopkeeper at Malans newsagents had accused Richard of stealing. He was innocent of the crime, but had been ordered off the premises nevertheless.

'They've got a right to protect their own goods, haven't they?' said Andrew.

'Don't see why. Everyone says half of their stuff's been nicked anyway.'

'That's just gossip,' protested Andrew.

'Well, why have the police been round twice already? They've only been open for three months. And how else can they pay such high wages?'

'Look, it's not our problem where the money comes from,' pleaded Andrew. 'We'd be just working there, minding our own business. Right? Come on!'

'No!' said Mark strongly. 'I'm not going to let Richard down just for a bit of extra money. I've never liked Malans, and I'm not going to work there. And you know what, you shouldn't work there either.'

'Why not?' asked Andrew.

'Once I went in there, and the shopkeeper offered to sell me cheap porno mags. It's just not right working for people like that.'

'That's not exactly the crime of the century, is it?' chuckled Andrew. 'So what if they're not perfect? We're not either. They're all right, especially their money. That's very all right. I think I will try for a job there.'

'It'll mean you'll have to give up this job.'

'That's no problem. I'll tell old man Brett when we get back.'

An equally cold morning a few weeks later found Andrew trudging towards Malans. He was a little late as he had waited to hear the cricket summary on the radio before he left. As he approached the shop, he looked up. Something was not quite right. The lights had not been turned on yet. Surely they hadn't overslept? He tried pushing the door open several times, before he noticed the small white card in the window. 'Closed. Moving to new premises.'

Dazed and crushed, Andrew wandered towards Brett's newsagent without meaning to. When he found himself outside the shop, he went in. Mr Brett was leaning over the counter. His angular features complemented his pleasant manner.

'Well, hello Andrew old chap,' he beamed.

'Hello,' Andrew replied faintly. Then, he collected himself and continued, 'Er, I suppose you've found a replacement.'

Mr Brett did not seem to understand, so Andrew carried on, 'My old job, could I have it back? I mean, is it vacant?'

'Afraid not,' said Mr Brett. 'No, I'm afraid it's gone. Boy took it just two days ago. Sorry old chap. Didn't know you wanted it back. What? Didn't think you said so.'

'No, I didn't,' whispered Andrew as he left the shop.

Suddenly he felt very alone and very poor.

Christine Strickett (16)
E. Finchley, London

The Good Mohican

The disco finished and Nicky started to walk to the bus stop.

Nicky was fifteen years old and had long, black hair and brown eyes. She hated coming home on her own, but her friends lived in the other direction and her Mum could not drive. Nicky's Dad had died in a car crash.

As she waited for her bus in the cold night air, she saw ten youths over on a spare piece of ground behind the bus stop. They looked a rough lot and Nicky hoped they would go away. As she looked she saw that they were punks, and that there were two groups. They were fighting and Nicky became very frightened. She hoped that her bus would soon come.

After a few minutes she looked round and realized that the youths had gone, except for two of them. They were standing, looking the other way at some bricks as if contemplating throwing them at someone.

Nicky turned round and stood in the shadows of the bus shelter, so as not to be seen by the two punks. She stood for what seemed like hours, but what was in fact about five minutes; then she heard the angry voices of the two punks. She crept further back into the shadows. As they walked past the bus stop, they caught sight of Nicky. The punks saw she was frightened so they decided to take their anger out on Nicky. They raped her, stole her clothes and all her money. Then, they dragged her on to the spare ground and left her there.

Nicky just lay there, hoping and praying someone would come and help her.

After a long while Nicky thought her prayers had been answered; she heard someone approaching. A vicar walked past and pretended not to see Nicky.

A few minutes passed and Nicky noticed her Member of Parliament crossing the spare ground. This time she cried out, hoping he would hear her and come and help. Alas, he did not have time to help girls who had been raped; he was late home from a meeting!

Nicky lay there for a long while, very cold and very hungry and thirsty. Then she saw the outline of a Mohican far away. She thought that if a vicar and her Member of Parliament would not help her, then a Mohican certainly would not.

As the Mohican approached, Nicky kept very still and quiet, so he would not see or hear her; but the Mohican did see her, and he went over to help her. He was very kind and he bandaged her wounds with his handkerchief and gave her his last can of beer. Then he wrapped her in his jacket, picked her up and took her to the nearest house, where he asked them to look after her.

The next day he came back and gave the couple who had looked after her his dole money.

Jane Rowland (14)
Stowmarket, Suffolk

Who Moved the Stone?

It seemed to the ancient and close-knit community of the small Italian village, San Aliquanto, that the huge and dominating boulder which rested, apparently immovable, high above the village on the top of Mount Ebola, had been placed there at the Creation. Indeed, even 'El Patri', a decrepit, white-haired and toothless old man, allegedly the founder of the village, could not give an explanation to account for the mystery. And so its presence had always been accepted and almost forgotten, taken for granted as part of the natural geography of the area, by the frisky villagers who lived each carefree day under its ominous shadow.

Recently, however, the potentially precarious position of the stone and the great destruction it might cause if dislodged had become obvious to the chubby and enormously proud Mayor of San Aliquanto, whose Town Hall would lie directly in the path of the tumbling and formidable rock. Frequent torrents of rubble had flowed down from the surrounding mountains and erratic earth tremors had shaken the village violently. Alarmed, he put himself to finding a solution to the problem.

The boulder lay balancing on the edge of a small plateau. Gradually, the plateau was declining in size as stone fell away on all sides and it was clear that one more tremor would be enough to tip its balance and send it crashing down the steep mountainside on to San Aliquanto. The Mayor proposed to his council that the boulder be dragged to the opposite edge of the plateau. Thus, at the next rumbling, the danger would disappear as the rock rolled harmlessly down the other side of the mountain. It was estimated to weigh roughly two tons. The council was confident that the combined strength of the fifty-six fit men of San Aliquanto would be sufficient to move it.

The following day the Mayor called for a meeting of all the villagers. When all were assembled, he silenced the general hubbub of curiosity with a sharp motion of the hand and, clearing his throat, began to outline the details of the frightening situation. Urgently he stressed to his shocked neighbours that the stone must be quickly moved. At the conclusion of his speech, his squeezed and high-pitched voice was shaking with worked-up excitement.

'Signors of San Aliquanto, if every able-bodied man comes and pulls – THE STONE WILL MOVE!'

It was not that his house and family were not in danger, but really Signor Apathé was not a man for energetic pursuits. True, he would go and hold the rope; not to do so would be considered a social crime by his neighbours, but when it came to pulling, he would only appear to be straining ferociously. Surely one man could not make the difference?

It was a peculiar sight; one hundred and twenty-six proud wives and screaming children and fifty-six men, closely packed on the tiny plateau of Ebola. The Mayor, raised commandingly over the crowd on a temporary plateau, coughed for attention. There was a tense hush.

'Gentlemen!' he squeaked. 'To your places!'

The men grimly took the rope.

'One . . . two . . . three . . . PULL!'

A great roar went up from the spectators as the glass of stillness and held breath was shattered.

Signor Apathé twisted his face, screwing up his eyes and mouth, and tried desperately to sweat.

'I hope it looks convincing,' he thought.

From the painful and wildly strained looks on each man's face, it looked as if they were trying to pull four tons.

And yet the stone did not move.

Guy Donegan-Cross (15)
Blackheath, London

The Picture

An old man had moved to a quiet country town, away from the noise of the modern city where he had lived. He soon settled down, enjoying the tranquillity of his new home, and found he liked nothing better than to have a leisurely cup of coffee at the café in the square and watch the world go by.

One day, he noticed a boy feverishly scrubbing the steps of a nearby house; later he saw him busy sweeping out a yard. Puzzled and amused to see such devotion to duty in one so young, he asked the café-owner about him. The man shrugged: the boy was after any work going, he even washed up sometimes at the café.

Intrigued by this information, the old man made a point of looking out for the boy. He spotted him in the most unexpected situations: mending fences, painting a dog's kennel, laboriously separating strands of wool for a lady knitting. At last the old man's curiosity got the better of him and, stopping the boy, he asked the reason for his industry.

'Well, sir, I'm saving up to buy a little picture that my mother admired. The one in that window. It's her birthday soon and I'm going to give it to her.'

Impressed by the solemnity of the boy's speech, the old man offered him some money to help reach his goal. The boy politely refused it, explaining that he would earn all the money needed.

The old man wandered over to the window and looked at the tiny square-framed painting, a watercolour of a wood in spring. Although the colours were slightly faded, the delicate spirit of spring remained, held captive by the artist's brush. No wonder the mother had liked it.

As the mother's birthday approached, the old man realized the boy could not possibly achieve his target, however hard he worked. He told the boy this but he just laughed and said he knew he would succeed. The old man was not so confident and when the fateful day arrived, he was reluctant to go for his usual coffee for fear of meeting the boy. He paused at the shop window to gaze at the picture. To his horror it was gone: sold that very day!

Suddenly he heard a cry behind him. Turning round, he saw the boy running to meet him. Words of clumsy comfort died on his lips as the boy explained how he had been able to buy the picture at last. He had been present when a small girl had fallen into the river. Everyone had stood still, horrified: then his limbs unfroze and, diving in, he dragged her to safety; her father had been so grateful, he had given the boy a reward for his bravery: this exactly matched the balance of the sum required.

'How wonderful!' exclaimed the old man.

'Not at all, sir,' the boy replied. 'I never doubted I would complete my task.'

Deborah Marshall (16)
Stamford, Lincolnshire

The 'Good' Samaritans

'Come on, Spurs!' shouted a gang of Spurs supporters as a player deftly took the ball up the pitch towards the goal.

'Shoot!'

'It's a goal!'

'We are the greatest!'

'What did you just say, mate?' bellowed an enormous man. 'I don't think I heard you right.'

From the blue and white scarf around his neck he was obviously a United supporter – and that meant trouble. David, who had shouted the offending remark, blushed, took a step backwards and began to stutter, 'I . . . I . . . er, said, it doesn't matter.' The big man realized he had scored a point and grinned at his friends, each one as menacing as the first.

As the match wore on it was plain, even to the most ardent United supporter, that Spurs were going to win.

John, watching the crowd in front, who grew more and more angry and began to abuse policemen, muttered to David, 'You should have stood up for yourself. We're going to beat them easily, and they know it!'

The largest swung round, glaring. 'Honestly Jack, I could have sworn I heard something squeak!'

'I said, we're going to win easily and . . .'

'I think he wants a fight!'

Soon there was chaos. Policemen were dragging people out of the mass of angry fighting maniacs. The United supporter, fearing big trouble from the law, had run, leaving the stands in disarray.

Later that evening a group of teenagers were walking along a road. One of the girls noticed a crumpled heap of blue and white, obviously an United supporter, lying by the road.

'There's someone here,' she shouted. 'He's hurt, badly I think.'

'Oh, Kate, leave him. Someone else will find him.'

'We'll be late.'

'You'll do more harm than good. He may have broken bones.'

Kate left the man's side. As she thought of all the complications that would be entailed in getting him to hospital, it did not seem such a good idea.

A short while afterwards a group of drunk Spurs supporters met the injured man. When they saw that he was an United fan they began to kick him and rub his face in the dirt.

The day dawned and the injured man grew weaker, the little life he had slowly ebbing away. Then John and David, the two boys who had been brutally injured by the United supporters, came along. When they saw the United scarf their first reaction was to cross over the road. Why should *they* help? But the boys, seeing that he was near to death, tried to drag him to the hospital for there was no telephone box nearby. Although they were both in pain they struggled on. At last they reached the hospital where all three men were admitted. Both John and David had bad injuries made worse by the long walk.

The United supporter recovered slowly. As soon as he had recovered consciousness, he was able to see the two boys who had saved his life.

'Thanks, mates. I . . . I . . . I'm sorry,' he said quietly.

'Don't mention it, anyone would have done the same,' they replied.

But would they?

Pippa McGowan (14)
Kingston-upon-Thames, Surrey

The Parable of the Cathedral

The kingdom of heaven is like a great cathedral, renowned the world over for its beauty and magnitude. Each year thousands of people visit it, but they have many different reasons for their visits.

Some come to study the architecture. They are interested only in the arches, the glowing stained-glass windows, the leering gargoyles, the carved pulpit and pews. They enjoy their fine surroundings, but they think of the cathedral solely as a stately building.

Some come to see just one detail – perhaps the tomb of a knight. They examine every aspect of it, noticing the Latin words, the dog at the knight's feet, the significance of the bend sinister on the shield. They do not look at all the other fascinating facets of the cathedral.

Some come because they have heard of it, and they want to see it for themselves. They hurry round, missing the most breathtaking details, so determined to find out why it is famous that they fail to observe its splendid unity. Afterwards they cannot understand why it is so admired.

Some come because they want to say that they have seen it.

They bustle round, worried that it will take more time than they have allowed on their carefully planned timetable. They know nothing of architecture, or religion, but explain everything to whoever happens to be standing nearby.

Some come because it is their church and they are expected to appear each Sunday morning. They stand, sit and kneel at the appropriate times, and mumble the responses of the service. They think of it only as a building they have to enter each week. They are concerned with the thought of lunch and their afternoon activities.

Some come to clean – to dust and to sweep. They, like those who come each Sunday, see it only as a building they must enter, for their jobs. They do not stop to think of the majesty of the cathedral.

Some come because they want to pray in magnificent surroundings. They envisage the cathedral as God's house. They come seeking serenity and beauty so that they can enjoy the perfect bliss of communicating with God. The sightseers are momentary interruptions in their prayers.

Many enter, but few know the entire beauty.

Those who study the architecture or the details see only the physical aspects and do not encounter God. Those who come because of its fame do not even see the true beauty. Those who come regularly also miss the beauty and spirit. But those who come to pray see the unique glory fully revealed – God and the beauty. It is they who are truly in Heaven.

Portia Spears (14)
Southampton, Hampshire

A Blanket of Faith

It was an average Wednesday night, Bill had gone to work at eight-thirty as usual. Bill was the man in charge at the local fire station, and was working on night shift. He didn't like night shifts much because there was never much action and the night always wore on boringly. But, although Bill didn't realize, tonight was going to be different.

Mr and Mrs Rogers were going out for their regular Wednesday-night bingo session and as usual had arranged for Barbara, their fourteen-year-old babysitter, to look after their three children: Samantha, who was six; Joey who was seven and a half; and Lisa, who was eleven years old. Barbara arrived at seven-thirty and was left in charge of the three children, who had been left with their parents' usual warning of: 'Behave yourselves for Barbara and make sure your sleeping-bags don't touch the heaters.'

The night wore on at the station and Bill was just about to have a sleep when the alarm was sounded. A young girl had sent in a phone call telling the brigade that the house where she was babysitting had gone up in flames after a blanket had fallen on to one of the heaters in a child's bedroom. She gave her name and address. It was then all systems go and the firemen rushed to the engine and quickly mounted and zoomed off to the scene of the fire.

When they got there they had soon set up their equipment and were ready to fight the fire.

The children and Barbara were sitting on the grass verge opposite the Rogers' house and were being comforted by neighbours. In all the fuss Barbara hadn't noticed six-year-old Sam slip away from them. As Barbara looked round she saw Sam dashing in through the door. She had gone back to the house to get Jemima, her favourite rag doll. Barbara quickly told Bill and he rushed up to the door only to be forced back by the flames. A few minutes ticked by as they wondered what to do. It was impossible to get in through the door or downstairs window as the fire had spread rapidly through the bottom of the house. As they looked up, they saw Sam at her bedroom window clutching the rag doll. She disappeared from the window only to return a few minutes later with a look of fear and horror on her face. She had obviously realized that she couldn't get out.

Bill rushed up with a ladder but couldn't get near enough to the bottom of the house to put it up. They shouted to Sam to open the window to give herself some air. When someone said that that would spread the fire, Bill answered sharply, 'Well, it may feed the fire but if that girl doesn't get some fresh air she'll die of suffocation.'

The firemen gathered together and decided that the only option left to them would be to have a blanket and get the girl to jump from the upstairs window on to the blanket. This was a frightening enough task for anyone let alone a small child. Bill got a loudspeaker and told Sam to stay calm and do as she was told. But it was no use, Sam couldn't bring herself to jump and was petrified. Bill tried in vain to coax her down and by this time

Mr and Mrs Rogers had arrived. Even they couldn't talk little Sam into jumping.

Suddenly Bill had a brainwave. He shouted up to the little girl, telling her to listen carefully and told her this. 'Sam, honey, I'll tell you what, you throw down Jemima first and we'll catch her. When you see that she's perfectly safe you can jump down yourself. You'll be all right – we'll catch you, I promise. Come on, there's a good brave girl.'

Sam shook her head and said not, but Bill talked to her and kept on persuading her until she finally agreed.

She threw down the doll, then after a bit more coaxing from Bill she closed her eyes and jumped. She landed safely in the blanket whereupon her mother rushed over and lifted her up, smothering her with kisses.

So Sam was saved simply by listening to Bill and by putting her faith and trust in him.

Lesley Cross (15)
Welshampton, Shropshire

Consideration

I used to live in a city slum; that was until one particular family forced us to move house. This was because they showed no consideration for other people.

We lived over the road from them, the Birches that is. Their family consisted of five people:

The father was a selfish man – thought only of himself. He worked at the sawmills. He went out drinking every night.

The mother a few years ago suddenly turned mental walking about the streets like a zombie.

The eldest daughter was mentally retarded. She was about eighteen years old.

The second eldest child was also a girl. She was a bright child, but suddenly she turned into a motorbike rocker and used to hang around with a motorbike gang. She played truant a lot.

The youngest child was a boy. He was aged about eleven; every other word he said was bad language.

One night they had a party at their house; crowds and crowds of people turned up. The music was heard all through the night. About four o'clock in the morning the motorbikes started to rev up and they made a terrible noise. So that very night my Dad got out of bed, put on his clothes and went storming out of the house. As it happens my bedroom window was opposite their house, and I could see what was going on. I suddenly caught sight of my Dad. He went running at these lads on motorbikes. He kicked one bike down. The rocker came at him, threw a punch. My Dad dodged the punch, then really quickly kicked the rocker between the legs. The rocker fell to the floor. Another jumped on my Dad's back, another leapt towards him. My Dad then furiously threw the rocker over his shoulder. He then attacked the third rocker, violently kicked him in the shin and punched him that hard he knocked him out.

Then just as suddenly as my Dad had appeared, he disappeared. The view fell silent; no one in sight.

The next day when I woke up, I didn't tell my Dad that I had seen him beat up the rockers. I just kept it quiet and surprisingly enough, he didn't say a word.

Meaning: If you don't show consideration for your friends you will lose them.

Carl Ayling (15)
Ellsemere, Shropshire

Trust

A little girl was born to a young couple who showed remarkable devotion to her. She was their first child and naturally they were very proud of her.

As the child grew up people noticed just what a pretty child she was. Before long she was attending school and proving to be quite intelligent.

Her parents, although very proud of her, were slightly worried. Often they would find her watching the television with squinted eyes or sitting in her bedroom, reading a book with the light on, when it was broad daylight.

Before long they decided that the best thing would be to take her along to the optician's. Just as they feared, the optician declared that the child's sight was slowly deteriorating. She was given glasses to help prevent too much strain but was told that she would have to read less and cut down on how much television she watched.

Now this came as a big blow to the child and her family. Day by day her sight would get worse, she would stumble over things in the house which normally she would avoid. She was wearing her glasses all the time but they did not seem to be making much difference any more. She became miserable and difficult to cope with. She could not come to terms with what was happening to her. She had now stopped attending school because her eyes were causing her a lot of bother.

Seeing her like this was tearing her parents apart. They could not stand to see this happening to their little girl who had had so much to live for.

So one day, in despair, the child's mother went to visit the doctor in an attempt to save the child's sight. The doctor pointed out that the child could have an operation but there were risks involved. If she did not have the operation, she would, in time, lose her sight; even having it there was always a chance that complications would arise. But there again she could come away cured.

The mother left the surgery with her mind in a turmoil. Her child meant so much to her, could she trust the doctors to operate successfully? She informed her husband of the conversation and spent the next couple of days with her mind in a daze. But she was not completely unaware of what was happening around her. The little girl was now getting frightened; her sight was faltering. This was just too much. Her mother decided then that the child would eventually go blind anyway, and an operation might give her a slight chance. She would just have to trust the doctors with her daughter's sight.

The operation was arranged and the little girl was taken into hospital. Very soon it was time for the operation to take place. Her mother gripped her daughter's hand as she was wheeled into the theatre, reassuring her that all would be well. But would it? Could the doctors save her sight?

It seemed to have been hours by the time the doctor eventually came out of the surgery. The mother ran to him, anxious for some news. He informed her that they had done all they could and that if she was cured they would find out in the next couple of days. The child was still asleep but her mother was able to go in and see her.

The child's progress was unbelievable. A few days later the bandages came off. She was cured, she could see. Her mother had trusted the doctors and they had cured her.

Alison Probert (16)
Shrewsbury, Shropshire

Trust

It was all quiet at 33, Beech Park and Tarquin and Cedric were quietly reading away in their bedroom. Tarquin sat up in bed and whispered across to Cedric: 'Have you been invited to the party that they're all going on about at school?'

'Whose party is this then?' he replied, with a wondering look on his face.

'Why, Claudia Smith's, stupid!'

'Oh, yes I have. Why, haven't you been invited or something?'

'Of course I have. Why do you think I asked? Anyway, I heard it's going to be a right rave-up so we are going to have to be careful when we go about asking Mum and Dad if we can go or not.'

'Yes, I suppose so, anyway let's get some sleep now and leave it until the morning.'

So they both put their books down and then settled down to sleep.

The morning came and Tarquin and Cedric rose from bed and went down to the kitchen for their breakfast. While they were sitting there eating their bacon and egg, Tarquin said to his Mum, 'Mum, Cedric and I have been invited to a party tonight at

Claudi   are going, do you think
we cou   P. 103 - 3

His   P. 104 - 5 - 5   and then said, 'Yes, but
on one   back home for eleven
o'clock   P 106 - 1   lcoholic.'

The   table and smiled at each
other.   ted their bags and made
their way to school.

All in all the day at school passed quickly and when they
arrived home they began preparation for the party. They had
their tea and then washed and changed. When seven o'clock
came round they said goodbye to their mother and she gave them
a last warning to be in for eleven o'clock and not to get drunk,
and then they set off.

When they arrived at Claudia's house they took their coats off,
and went into the living-room to dance. The night soon passed
and when they came to come home Tarquin wouldn't go and he
was drunk, so Cedric left without him.

When Cedric reached home he explained to his Dad that
Tarquin had had too much to drink and wouldn't come home. So
their Dad set off to fetch Tarquin and within ten minutes he was
back with him.

During the evening Tarquin was violently sick and his Mum
and Dad had to keep getting up to him and this made them a lot
angrier.

One month later Cedric asked if he could go to a friend's party
and he was allowed to go but when Tarquin asked he was not
allowed, because of the way he had behaved at the previous
party.

Simon Metcalfe (16)
Ellesmere, Shropshire

Peacemakers

Down our road there are two families, living a few houses away from each other, and they are having a major row over a minor car accident, which involved their cars.

Mr Jones who lives at number ten, has a son who was involved in the accident. Mr Jones's son, John, is in love with Sally Peters, the daughter of the other family involved in the crash. Because of this row Sally and John were not able to see each other.

They have tried to meet each other in secret, but their families were getting very over-protective about their children and they won't allow them out of their sight. So John and Sally were finding it very hard to see each other.

One day the Jones family had to go out and John said that he felt ill so they had to leave him at home. When the Jones family had gone John phoned Sally up and was very surprised to hear that she was at home all by herself. During the telephone conversation John asked Sally if she would marry him. He told her that they could go off for a week, get married and then when they returned their families would be talking to each other. Sally told John that she would marry him.

Within half an hour John was round at Sally's house with his case packed in the boot of the car. He helped Sally with her cases and then got into the car and drove off, leaving a note to tell their parents not to worry.

When Mr Jones came back and saw that John's car had gone he began to get worried because he had not mended the brakes and the steering was on its way out. He quickly went into the house and found Mrs Jones crying. When he asked her what she was crying for she handed him a note which read:

Dear Mum,

I have run away to get married to Sally Peters. I would have told you but I knew you would not allow me to marry her because of this stupid car crash. I will be back in a week to collect my things.

John

Mr Jones then told his wife about the car and that he had not finished mending the brakes. After he had calmed Mrs Jones down the phone rang and it was Mr Peters saying that Sally had left home leaving a note, which told Mr Peters that she had run away with John to get married.

Mr Jones asked Mr Peters if he would like to go around to his house to try and work something out. Mr Peters and his wife went to the Jones's house and this time instead of blaming each other as they had done in the car crash they were blaming themselves, saying how stupid they had been.

Mr Jones and Mr Peters went out in their cars to all the hotels and register offices that they could think of and not one of them had heard about Sally or John. When they returned home, both of their wives were looking very worried. This was because they had received a phone call from a hospital in London saying that a Mr and Mrs J Jones were in a crash, because the brakes had failed on their car. However, both of them were only suffering from bruises and John had got a broken arm. The hospital suggested that they went to the hospital to pick up the two injured people.

When they reached the hospital they were so glad to see each other that they forgot that they were in the middle of a major row.

When everyone arrived home they all were very friendly with each other, and John and Sally were soon living in a place of their own.

The meaning of this story about the peacemakers is that you should forgive people if they do wrong to you, because if you don't, you could make other people, who are very close to you, angry with you, and you might upset them.

Caroline Ankers (15)
Ellesmere, Shropshire

The Holiday of Sin

Mike had just left school, and had been invited to go and stay with friends. They had made a fully planned weekend; Mike had said he would go if his father let him. He was allowed to go, if he behaved, even though his father did not approve of his friends.

Mike left early on Friday evening and arrived at his friends' about 11.30 pm. They were staying at Paul's cottage in the country. 'Hi Mike,' said Paul as Mike popped his head around the door. 'I see you managed to persuade the old man to let you come then.'

'He fell for the made-up plan then,' said Paul's brother Greg.

'Yeh, he asked a few searching questions, but being the genius I am, I coped,' replied Mike with a grin across his face.

They turned out their sleeping-bags and lay talking to each other, sometimes dropping off to sleep. Two o'clock arrived and they collected the equipment they needed for the robbery. They were going to break into a large TV shop. They left the cottage for the half-hour journey to town. They had arranged to meet a couple of Paul's other friends there at three o'clock, but after waiting until half-past they decided to break in without them. After successfully breaking in, they took a portable TV, a twenty-six-inch remote control, and a Sony video recorder, leaving the sign they had decided on (a broken black heart), where they had taken the TVs from.

They arrived at the cottage at 6.12 a.m., very happy and excited that they had succeeded even without the other two friends. They drank whisky to celebrate and then retired to their sleeping-bags for a good morning's sleep.

They were woken up by the postman knocking at the door. They immediately thought it was the police so they started to panic. But when they discovered it was the postman they relaxed. He had brought a large parcel for them and also a letter. They were addressed to Paul's Mum so they pushed it to one side and left it. They hid the TVs up in the cottage's loft, and then ate brunch.

Mike wrote a note home to his father saying he was staying with his friends for an extra two months. They continued to break in to small places, for example, electrical shops, garages, until a week before they were about to leave Paul came up with the idea of robbing a bank. Everyone else thought it was ridiculous but Paul wanted to go through with it and made all the plans.

'What happens if we get caught?' said Mike, the night before the robbery.

'We'll act as though we're drunk and give them their money back,' said Paul.

After a long discussion it was decided they'd do the break-in, if Paul did all the work while the others watched. They succeeded in stealing fifty thousand pounds and the next evening in the newspaper they discovered they had hit the headlines.

Two days after, Mike, Paul and Greg moved back home. Mike's Dad was angry with Mike for staying on with his friends.

'I hope you didn't get into trouble. Remember, I trusted you,' said Mike's Dad.

'You knew you could trust me. I would never get into trouble,' replied Mike.

After being home three days police started to appear more than usual. A few days later Paul, Mike and Greg were arrested for bank robbery. When they were asked about how they got the information the police replied: 'Paul and Greg Buller's younger brother heard Paul arranging it over the telephone before they left for the so-called holiday.'

After a court case where they were found guilty, Mike's Dad was very angry and shouted: 'I trusted you, you let me down. Well I tell you this, Mike, I will never trust you again.'

Diane Whitfield (16)
Ellesmere, Shropshire

The Day a Soldier Died

This story is all about a lad whose name was Bob Evans. He lived in Norwich, down in East Anglia. He was twenty years of age and his mother was dead, so he lived with his father.

Ever since he was about ten years of age his ambition was to join the army and fight for his country, even though his father disagreed.

Anyway, now he thought he could do that because he was twenty, so he told his father and his father said: 'You do what you want.' This was his chance to join the army.

The next day he went into town to pay a visit to the army careers office. He saw a man who was in charge of the force and he told Bob that he seemed to be the right sort of lad who could make a career in the army. Bob knew he was getting closer to joining, then it was left at that and Bob returned home.

He arrived home and his father was asleep so Bob didn't disturb him, he went up to his bedroom.

Some weeks passed and Bob hadn't heard anything from the army, then one morning a letter came and it told him that he had been chosen for an interview on 10 September 1981. Bob jumped up in the air with delight; his father also was very delighted.

On the day of the interview Bob was very nervous. His father wished him good luck and Bob left for his interview. When he got there he saw a different man than before, but he was still just as nice. It lasted about fifteen minutes and the man told him that they would let him know if he had got the job. Then Bob left.

He waited for weeks and weeks again like he had waited for his interview, but eventually a letter came and it said that he had been accepted into the army and would start his first posting in Northern Ireland after his training. Bob was delighted.

A few more weeks passed and it was time for him to leave. He said goodbye to his father and left.

He arrived in Ireland some months later; he was about to begin his first posting in the army.

For the first couple of days Bob was very nervous, but eventually he made many friends even though he went around carrying a gun. Then the day came that he had to kill someone. It was a middle-aged man who had shot his mate, so Bob shot him. It took time for him to recover, but he did.

Six months passed and he had seen quite a lot of terrible things in Ireland.

The day came, however, when Bob was shot and killed in the course of his duties.

Bob's body was brought back to Norwich and there he was buried with full military honours. This was the end of a soldier who had sacrificed his life trying to keep law and order in Northern Ireland.

Andrew Jones (15)
Ellesmere, Shropshire

A Hijacked Plane

I boarded the plane to Malta. I was going to meet my boyfriend who was already there. As I boarded the plane I started talking to a young girl who looked no more than nineteen or twenty whose name was Suzanne. When we were on the plane I got talking to this girl more and I found out that she was three months pregnant, and was going to her husband's parents' home to stay until her baby was born.

The plane took off and headed for Malta. The pilot said that the flight would take about five hours, from the airport where we took off, which was London.

We had been flying for about two hours, when this young lad stood up and started shouting, then out of his briefcase he got a hand grenade, and he held this in his hand and he started waving his hand around like anything so that he made sure that everyone could see what he was holding, and so not to make any sudden moves. Then he took out the pin of the hand grenade and threw it on the floor, and so if he took his hand off it, the whole plane would blow up. All the passengers were calmed down, while the young man made his way to the cockpit. Anyway when he was there Suzanne became hysterical and had to be comforted. Then the pilot came out and informed us that we were being diverted to Germany on the hijacker's orders.

As we were flying to Germany the weather seemed to get really bad; the rain came down really hard pelting against the windows and the clouds became lower and so you couldn't see anything outside. Suzanne became more upset and she told me that she was really frightened. I tried to reassure her and said that everything would be OK. Every now and then the air hostesses said how long we were away from Germany – it seemed like for ever. We found out that the hijacker had been in the war which took place at the Falkland Isles a few months ago, and that he kept remembering things like his friends getting tortured and sometimes himself and now he is mentally disturbed in the mind, and for some reason he wanted to go to Germany.

By the time we were at Germany the aeroplane nearly ran out of fuel. When we landed in Germany it was pouring down with rain. To get off the plane we had to slide down an inflatable which was like a chute, and the men had to hold it at the bottomn and all of the passengers had to trust the men that they would catch them at the bottom, especially Suzanne being three months pregnant. When all the passengers were off they were rushed to hospital.

When the hijacker came off the plane he was shot dead and the hand grenade was found to be a fake one. Suzanne's baby was found not to be harmed.

This was about Trust. In this parable all the passengers had to trust the hijacker not to blow up the plane and they also had to trust the men on getting them safely off the plane.

Tina Rogers (15)
Ellesmere, Shropshire

Home Sweet Home

Mrs Frost opened her eyes and smiled. She was not sure where she was but she felt strangely unconcerned.

She was lying in a small white room, at one end of which was a small door.

The last thing she remembered was standing in her kitchen; she had felt a pain in her head; after that all was blank.

The door swung open and a man clothed in white robes entered.

He smiled. 'I am St Peter. You are, my dear, in heaven. I know you may find it hard to accept but, welcome to heaven. In a short while I will take you to your home.'

Mrs Frost frowned. 'My house?'

'Yes, everyone in heaven has a house. You see, for every kind word you said on Earth we gave you a brick towards your house and for every good deed you did we gave you a flower for your garden. Do you see that?'

Mrs Frost nodded (though she was still confused). What sort of house would she get?

'You see, some people have large houses and others have small ones.'

St Peter led Mrs Frost through the small door and out into a large street. Every house was like a palace. They turned a corner and St Peter explained that the first house on the left would be Mrs Frost's.

When they reached the house, Mrs Frost stared in horror at the sight which met her eyes. Her house was a heap of rubble. Crumbled brick and dead flowers lay everywhere.

Mrs Frost was heartbroken. 'Look, I was good on Earth. I was nice to people. Don't I deserve better than this?'

St Peter sighed. 'I am afraid that this house crumbled because of you.' He paused. 'Before I met you I checked the computer to find out about your life. It seems that you did many good things on Earth. But, for a reward. If there wasn't something in it for you then you weren't interested. Is that true?'

Mrs Frost nodded.

'Well, when we built your house we built a fine dwelling because you had said and done many good things. Though not sincerely. But, I am afraid it crumbled. The quality of your house is a reflection of your life's quality. Because you never helped anyone spontaneously you had few friends. Your life's quality, like the bricks' quality, was poor, and so your house crumbled. It is no good being nice to people if you don't truly mean it. Now, don't worry too much. There are plenty of nice people about. I am sure they will help you. Good luck.'

He disappeared around the corner.

Mrs Frost realized everything he had said was true. She had expected a glorious palace. Now she was left with a heap of crumbled brick and a few dead flowers. She lay back on the ground, the rough grass tickling her back. A smile played across her lips and soon she was laughing. Laughing at the world.

Francesca Furlong (14)
Wroxham, Norfolk

A Parable of the Future

There was once a beautiful valley in an undeveloped part of Russia. Throughout summer the sun beat down on the ripening corn, which made a stunning contrast with the dark green valley pastures.

Mechanical farm machines had not yet reached this hidden part of the world and most of the labour was done by man. One such man was Werner Doodrove. He was a cheerful man who always smiled and was very polite, despite his very hard life.

Another man lived in the valley. He was called Johan Martovlov, and like Werner he had a wife and three children and had to work where Werner worked, in the fields, very hard to make a living.

One day a man came to the village in the valley in a motor car from Moscow. The children that were playing, half-dressed in rags, stopped their play and ran round and round this strange machine of which they had never seen the like before.

All the workers came from the fields. Werner too left his work and went to the village square. They announced that machines were being sent to the village and how new methods would be used to farm the land.

Werner left the square; things were going to get better, he thought. Johan also thought, not of the people but of the fact that he would become richer.

Machinery came into the village, and after three years Werner had become very rich, as the head of the village. Johan also was now rich, but his wealth was obtained from exploiting the people.

One summer's morning Werner was in a field looking over the land, when he saw Johan also out. Suddenly a white light appeared to the two of them and God spoke to them: 'Werner, you please me; Johan, repent or I shall take away your wealth and family.'

They were stunned, but Johan managed to speak: 'I shall never repent,' and with those words he ran off.

Two days later a mysterious plague went through the village and everyone recovered except Johan's family who all died. Johan was mad and took revenge by killing Werner's eldest son and then he left the area.

Five years passed and Werner had become even more rich and powerful and had done a great deal for the village. It was the end of the harvest and Werner looked out across the fields, happy that all the work was done. Then across the field came a shape. Werner watched it come closer then realized it was Johan.

'Johan, you have returned; welcome brother.'

'Thank you Werner, I have been in the wilds and have repented.'

Then God spoke: 'You have both pleased me. You Werner, for – despite your power – forgiving Johan, and you Johan for truly repenting.'

God will forgive you if you are truly sorry, but when you are wealthy do not be like Johan and let greed make you evil, but be like Werner who despite his wealth and power still knew that

God was his master and did everything for the good of the people and therefore was a better man in the eyes of God.

Matthew Large (15)
Darlington, County Durham

Make the Most of What Life Offers!

Once upon a time, in a town like my own, there was a school, and in that school there was a class who sat listening to the teacher. She was talking about Christianity and how the Word had been spread centuries before by Jesus's disciples.

At the front of the class sat the interested pupils; at the back sat the bored ones, slouched, scribbling rude comments on the desks. The teacher often stopped and asked the lazy pupils to listen but inwardly she knew it was quite useless. They had once been attentive but now were at the age when nothing in life mattered and they claimed Christianity to be an 'immature' belief.

Suddenly a pupil walked into the room and told the teacher that the headmistress urgently wanted to see her. So, reluctantly, she told the class to split into two groups to discuss the prospects for Christianity in Britain in the next fifty years.

The serious pupils welcomed this and sensibly formed a circle with their notepads open. They all had interesting points to make and very soon a discussion was under way, everyone listening to the others' thoughts and ideas.

The uninterested pupils, however, regarded the teacher's

absence as the ideal opportunity to relate the happenings of the evening before. Soon there were paper aeroplanes across the floor, slogans on the blackboard, girls running around the room and a boy teasing one of the conscientious pupils for his keen interest in Christianity.

Within a few minutes the teacher had returned, horrified at the uproar in her classroom, and her horror turned to anger when she read the blackboard. She needed no explanation; she could tell by the faces of the troublemakers exactly who was responsible.

When she had restored order in the room they turned back to the topic of the afternoon. The teacher asked those who had considered the problem for their notes and was very pleased by their response. Then she asked the other group what they had written. They were not in the least worried at what the teacher would say to them. When the truth was revealed and she found out that they had done no work at all she almost exploded. She finally sent them to the headmistress who severely reprimanded them for not being able to conduct good behaviour while the teacher had temporarily left the room.

'I tell you now, every one of you that wastes the time given to you and your talents, shall only regret it. If you live like the stupid group you shall find no reward or satisfaction from life, only punishment and mockery.

'But those among you who act as the wise group did and make use of your talents, however useless you may think them to be, shall find praise, enjoyment and self-satisfaction from what you have done in life!'

Alison Ash (15)
Weymouth, Dorset

Green Papers

The sun shone on to the pavement and was reflected like a sheet of gold from the window panes. One man walked down the street towards the tall grey building, which was the bank. He walked past the travel agent's, past the Oxfam centre, and past the supermarket. He stood impatiently waiting for the doors to open unaware of the washed and well-worn appearance of his coat, but clutched the old leather case in which the previous night's takings were stocked. He entered into the bank, pushing to the front of the crowd, and by means of several discourteous remarks to the cashier, deposited the notes into his bank account.

The windows of the room were dirty and the room itself, though fairly large, was old and poorly heated. That night he went to sleep and dreamt that he was in a strange land, a misty and cloudlike expanse. In the distance he saw a light and went shuffling towards it holding his old leather case tightly, he pushed through a group of people and banged his case down on the desk holding the sign 'Chief Cashier'.

'Yes,' said the bespectacled man seated in front of him. 'Have you come to settle up?'

'Yes,' answered the man, suddenly humbled by this ageless

figure before him. He opened the case and laid the crisp notes on the desk.

The cashier looked amused and laughed. 'Is this a joke?'

'No,' answered the surprised man.

'Come on, you don't expect to pay back the loan of life with pieces of green paper do you?'

'Well yes,' answered the man, very confused.

'Oh I see you've forgotten the terms?' came the cashier's reply. 'Well let me outline the main points of our agreement. My boss doesn't ask much, no interest, only that you can change the loan into a more profitable form of return, i.e. experiences, generosity, goodwill, joy, service, etc., but I'm afraid we don't take pieces of green paper, so perhaps we can forget our little misunderstanding and get down to business.'

The man protested: 'But this is ridiculous, my money is perfectly good.'

The cashier remained calm. 'All right, all right, so things are a bit down at the moment. Why didn't you say so? Look, I'm not ungenerous and I'll give you an extension of three years.'

With that he found himself sitting upright in his bed and for the first time the next day saw the travel agent's, the church, the Oxfam shop and the friendly cashier at the bank in a new light.

Mandy Ryan (16)
Rainhill, Merseyside

Red Hands

It was the second day of the week beginning June, hot and sultry, as Fred Small, a middle-aged joiner, plump in appearance and going bald, limped in the direction of the car park. He passed a flower border highlighted by white lilies, blue delphiniums, roses, paenies, yellow achiellea, tulips and colourful antirrhinums, wiping away the pearls of sweat that lay on his forehead. Small was a reserved, quiet, unsocial individual. He lived alone in a small house left to him by his Aunt Veronica, and had a housekeeper, a tall, slim, mysterious woman, with long black hair whom he neither liked nor got on with.

Now, as he approached his old brown Mini, all he wanted to do was drive home and take a long, cool shower. Unlocking the car door he noticed a bit of paper on the ground. He crouched down to pick it up. Overweight and unfit, he held on to the car door; then when he had picked up the paper he heaved himself up with tremendous difficulty, still holding on to the door.

He climbed into the car, taking several deep breaths, then unfolded the piece of paper. What he saw made his heart stop beating, then beat like that of a drum, alternately. It was a cheque made out for £40,000 cash. Tempted easily, Small decided to keep it.

He started the car and half an hour later Small was standing by his garden gate. He quickly limped up the stone path and headed towards his bedroom where he would put away the cheque that was in his pocket, and take that long-awaited shower before the housekeeper called him for tea. In his room he slammed the door shut, walked to the connecting bathroom, and switched on the shower, thus drowning the sound of hoovering which the housekeeper had begun in the next room. He removed his clothes, laid them in a neat, tidy pile on the bed, took his shower and later returned feeling cool and relaxed. He then changed his trousers and went to eat tea. The remainder of the day was spent in his workshop varnishing an old stool and thinking of the cheque.

A cool breeze wafted past him as he lay awake the next morning in bed. He had been up since dawn thinking of the cheque and had at last decided on all the wonderful things he was to do with it. First he would receive the greatest of pleasure by giving his housekeeper the sack. Then he'd give in his notice at work, book a holiday abroad, perhaps sell his house and buy another one in the country, purchase a new workshop consisting of all the latest tools etc., visit a health farm to try and lose some weight, have a row of servants who'd . . .

Hazel Bent walked into the bank, smiling. She handed a cheque to the young man behind the counter, stating that she would like to have it cashed. As she walked out of the bank carrying her £40,000 she thought of her once-upon-a-time employer, his carelessness, her fruitfulness, how she was going to spend the money. She was met by a ray of golden sunshine . . .

Dawn Crookes (16)
Wirksworth, Derbyshire

The Boast and the Race

'Where are you going at this time of night?' screamed Peter's mother from the lounge as the front door slammed. The answer to her question came with the revving of a motor bike. 'Oh not again! He'll kill himself one of these days,' she exclaimed peevishly.

'Keep it down, can't you woman. I'm trying to watch the match,' muttered her husband.

Mrs Cuthbert opened a curtain slightly and peered out into the murky darkness. There was no sign of a motorbike and the sound of one speeding down St Saviour's Drive had all but disappeared.

The door of the Dolphin pub burst out and Peter swaggered in and sat down on a chair next to four youths who were dressed, like him, in leathers. 'Knew it was yer bike, soon as I 'eard the cranky sound,' Rod laughed.

'It's not cranky,' exclaimed Peter indignantly.

'It's not a bit cranky,' mocked the others.

'Don't get so touchy, Pete. Rod was only 'aving you on. C'mon, it's your round,' said Steve lazily.

After a few beers, Peter became increasingly irritable. 'My bike's not cranky,' he slurred. 'Better 'n yours anyway.'

'Kid can't hold his beer,' muttered Rod slyly.

'All right, boy! Let's have a race.'

'Rod,' said Steve, 'you know you're faster than Pete . . . and you know what 'appened last time!'

'I can race him anyday,' shouted Peter.

'You're on!'

'OK!'

The two jumped up and walked out of the door. Outside the night was chill. It sobered Peter up a bit and he began to feel uneasy about his boast but one look at Rod made him change his mind.

'Well, Pete, let's see who's the fastest,' said Rod scornfully.

The two raced off into the night. Gradually, Rod began to overtake Peter. Peter became angry and accelerated hard, but it was no use, Rod was overtaking him.

Suddenly, as he turned a corner, he saw a car coming straight towards him. He swerved, as did the car. The last thing he remembered was a blinding flash and a sharp pain in his leg.

'And how are you feeling today?' said a nurse.

Pete opened his eyes and saw he was in a hospital. 'Oh, my leg,' he cried, screwing his eyes up in pain.

'I'm afraid it's badly broken,' said the nurse.

'I saw a car swerve . . .' said Peter weakly.

He saw the nurse's face fall. 'I'm afraid the car that swerved . . . the girl driving . . .' She left the sentence unfinished and turned away.

Peter lay back weakly. A girl had died because of his boastfulness and stupidity. 'I'll never boast again,' he said aloud but his words were hollow.

A girl had died and it was his fault.

Anna Griffiths (14)
South Woodham Ferrers, Essex

Forgiveness

It was a warm summer's day and Matthew, the son of a farmer, was working in his field, for he was very independent, and he was also very kind.

He lived in an old run-down house at the edge of the wood, for he had no wife to look after it. He did most domestic things himself. He looked after his house and himself, as well as tending to his sheep and ploughing and planting his fields. He had a few labourers to help him, but not many because he just didn't have the money to pay them.

He had a brother called Benjamin. He lived just the other side of the wood. Now Benjamin was a very mean and unkind person. He got other people to do all his jobs. He made them cook, and clean the house and he also made them plough and plant his fields; he paid them meanly.

Now one day Benjamin went to visit his brother, for all his labourers had walked out on him. He asked Matthew to help him plant a field of potatoes. Being a kind person Matthew left all his work to go and help his brother. They got to his brother's house and set to work. After just twenty minutes Benjamin cried out in pain. Matthew rushed over to see what was the matter. Benjamin said he had a pain in his chest and would have to go and lie down and have a rest. So Matthew helped his brother home and laid him down to rest, then off he went to finish off planting the potatoes. By the end of the day he was very tired.

The next day he woke up to the sound of somebody hammering the door down and shouting. Matthew stepped out of bed and opened the door. A burst of sunlight flooded in. In the bright light stood Benjamin, he insisted that he get dressed and hurry to his house. Matthew quickly got dressed and went round to his brother's house.

When he got there what a sight met his eyes. Half the house roof had fallen through. His brother begged him to mend it, but he was afraid he couldn't help as he still wasn't feeling very well. So Matthew did it himself. It took him all day and half the night to finish it, while his brother sat and watched him.

Matthew was worn out. When he went home he went straight to bed.

The next day he awoke very late, he was still a bit tired from the previous day. He got dressed and went to work in his own fields.

Meanwhile, at his house, Benjamin was laughing about how he had tricked Matthew into working for him. He decided to go and call on his brother to see if he could trick Matthew into doing any more jobs for him.

On his way he collapsed and there he lay for days. You see no one used that road much. They found him four days later. It was too late, he was already dead.

Matthew knew that his brother had been tricking him into working for him, but he was so kind he didn't say anything. That night Matthew sat down and prayed. He prayed to God to ask forgiveness for Benjamin. He asked God to forgive all the wrong and nasty things his brother had done. For it was his brother and he loved him, no matter what he had done.

Claire Graham (15)
Bottesford, Scunthorpe

Change of Heart

The pouring of the rain hitting against the window made the sad girl very unhappy. A part of her was never there. The girl was unhappy because she was fat. At school she had nicknames. Making the school days very uneasy. She would run out of a lesson because of this. Her mother is ashamed of her but does not admit it to her daughter. When she talks to other mothers she never mentions her daughter Tina.

Tina knows that her mother is ashamed of her and cries herself to sleep at nights under the covers. Tina wishes she had never been born. Why did she have to be fat? Why did her mother feel ashamed of her? Tina is a human being just like any other person in this world.

Tina had only one good friend who made her happy. This was an old lady living on an estate at the back of the shops. Tina grabbed her coat and ran out in the dark, the rain going in her face and blinding her eyes. When Tina arrived at the door of the lady, she knocked. The lady opened the door. Tina went in and they talked. Tina told the lady why she was very unhappy. She told the lady that the world was not meant for her.

Deep down in Tina there was some reasoning, but she had

never known of this, until this moment. The lady got her stick, which enabled her to move to an old drawer. The lady opened the drawer and brought out some photos.

The photos are of a fat girl about fifteen years of age. The lady told Tina that it was she when she was Tina's age. She was a fat girl just like Tina. Then another photo was shown when the lady was eighteen years of age. She had a slim figure and was very good-looking. This gave a smile and great lift to Tina.

The lady explained to Tina how she became slim. She ate less and went to a diet class. This made Tina determined to go on a diet and change her life. Knowing that she would be a lot happier, Tina went home, keeping the whole thing a surprise.

After school she would go to a diet class every night. Tina began to feel better and feel slimmer. It was a great sensation for Tina.

Days and weeks went by and she eventually lost the amount of weight she needed to lose. Tina's mother could see a change in Tina.

Then on one night after diet class Tina told her mother that she had been on a diet. Tina's mother could not believe it. She had a very slim figure and clothes which were in fashion. Tina's mother cried and told Tina to forgive her for being ashamed.

Her mother told Tina that she was sorry for the love she did not give her. In the house in which they lived there was a new beginning. For respecting and loving each other. But most of all the forgiveness.

Wendy Trippitt (15)
Scunthorpe

A Miserable Christmas

I lay on my bed, staring up at the ceiling and feeling very miserable. At first I could not understand why I felt so depressed, then it suddenly struck me – it was December the twenty-fifth. How could I bear it? Spending Christmas Day with a bunch of old ladies was not my idea of a happy Christmas.

It all went back to a month ago, when I heard my Uncle in church, asking if anyone who would be spending Christmas Day alone would like to spend it at his house. My heart sank, that would totally ruin Christmas for me. I normally spent the day at my Uncle and Aunty's house. It had always been an extra special occasion which I looked forward to. The house was a very large Victorian one, and when it was decorated for Christmas it looked really lovely. Outside the front door would be a huge Christmas tree, which was lit up at night. Inside, in the largest room, there would be another tree, and in the evening we would sing carols around it, with just the lights of the tree on. It was quite magical, but now it was ruined! I would not have my Aunty and Uncle to myself.

The alarm went off, and I realized that if I was quick, I might just get my Aunty and Uncle to myself for an hour. I arrived at ten-thirty in the morning. The guests were not going to arrive until eleven-thirty, so it looked as if my wish might be granted. This was not to be; the doorbell rang within the first ten minutes. I could not believe it, and as I watched eight old ladies troop in, my precious hour flew out of the window. By eleven-fifteen they had all arrived. I had presumed that there would be about ten or fifteen. When I finished counting, I arrived at the grand total of thirty-five. This did not include my family, my Aunty and Uncle's family, nor all the children. There were rather a lot of children, and they ranged from a screaming toddler to very energetic ten-year-olds.

At first I sat on my own feeling very sorry for myself, but as this became increasingly morbid, I decided to join in with the general buzz of conversation. As they were all so happy and excited, I started to cheer up too, and it seemed only a few minutes before we were all being ushered into the one room for dinner. Oh no, I thought, here comes the crunch, war-time rationings. How wrong I was. There was quite a lot to get through and, by the time I had finished, I was on the point of bursting. So was everyone else, but this did not deter them from causing a total uproar with the crackers. First there were wild screams as the crackers popped and banged all over the room. Then there were 'oohs' and 'aahs' as they admired one another's paper crowns. Finally there was a most hideous racket as they danced in and out of the room, blowing their plastic whistles!

The afternoon passed far too quickly, and even though some of the conversations were a little boring, as long as they were enjoying themselves, it just did not seem to matter. Dinner had hardly gone down before we were told that tea was on the table. The old ladies quickly said that they were starving and began to clear the table. I have never seen old people eat so much in my life, nor in such a manner – they 'wolfed' it down! It was not just a case of second helpings, they had four or five! Nothing was wasted, and my Aunty's two little dachshunds kept the floor clear of crumbs.

After tea we all squashed ourselves into one room for carol singing. This was a bit difficult as there were rather a lot of us, but by now I just could not be bothered about whether I had a seat or not, as I was so happy. After singing virtually every carol at least twice, one car arrived to take some of them home. Gradually more followed, leaving everyone only a little time to say goodbye.

Realizing that it was time to go, they all became a little sullen and quiet, no one really wanting to get their coats on. Slowly they began to start looking for their coats. I opened the door to find a few coats, and what a sight met my eyes. Seated on the rocking-horse, hat on head, and blowing a whistle, was an old lady. However, she was not just sitting there quietly, she was rocking that horse wildly, so much that she became rather dangerous.

Seeing the fun she was having, the others quickly queued up for a ride, all riding very precariously, and only just hanging on!

The car drivers were getting rather impatient, so we tried to pack a few of them in. This was harder than it seemed for just as you finished loading the back seat, the one in the middle would suddenly remember that she had left a glove behind, or that she hadn't said goodbye. Ten minutes later, we would find her back on the rocking-horse, or playing carols on the organ – in fact, anything just to stay a little longer!

When the house had finally been emptied, there was a notice-able quietness everywhere; and somehow it didn't seem quite right. Although it had been a bit hectic, it had certainly been fun and the old people had enjoyed their Christmas for once.

Although I had lost my Christmas Day in one way, simply by making these people happy, I had had the best Christmas possible.

Karen Brocklesbury (18)
Bromsgrove, Hertfordshire

The Greedy Child

Memories of my childhood seem so like the realities of our world today.

Mother would buy me the toys I had longed for. Suddenly, there would be no place in my life for these toys. I had now seen something else – something better – but most of all, something all my friends had, which made my new toy seem so old.

'Never ever satisfied,' I would be told, 'never content with what you have.'

Every day I longed for something new, my thoughts always set on the property of other people. I just couldn't understand why Mother wouldn't buy me all these things.

As the days passed, I noticed myself wanting more and more things. It became like a need to have everything everyone else had. The greed and selfishness grew so strong that they changed my character.

I was growing up fast and found myself wanting less. Teenage maturity had hit me with a bang. Dating boys, going to parties and smoking had taken over my life.

Now I have passed that stage and have a family of my own, I look back on my cruel childhood and compare it with today's world. Not more than fifteen to thirty years ago, a certain country developed the H-bomb. Immediately the race began. Every country wanted this bomb. No one wanted to be left out. They had to have what other countries had. No matter at what price, they wanted the bomb. They took the money out of the citizens' pockets by raising taxes, increasing food prices, doubling rent and rates, selfishly thinking only of their power. The people were crying out for mercy, no longer able to afford, in most cases, even the necessities of life, let alone the luxuries. Barely scraping for survival, the inhabitants rebelled. It was like 'ROB the POOR and GIVE to the RICH'. The governments were determined to obtain the H-bomb.

After years of toiling they achieved their aim. They thought of peace and restoring their nations. Before long, though, they were running the race all over again as a couple of countries had been working on improving their weapon when they came up with something NEW – BIGGER – BETTER – The Nuclear Missile.

Russia competed with America to see who had the best space shuttle and who could send people to the moon first. The whole world now seems to be competing with itself. Everyone wants what other people have. They want theirs to be better than everyone else's.

Will this world and its inhabitants never be satisfied with what they have? It would save a lot of time and trouble if everyone was satisfied and content with what was theirs.

There is an old saying which goes, 'You want and want but cannot get – You get and get but do not want.'

Sherlyn Christopher (17)
Wembley, London